Modi-fied India

An analysis of India's transformation in Modi era

Ravi Ranjan

Modi-fied India

Copyright © 2019 by Ravi Ranjan

Ravi Ranjan
Väderkvarnsgatan 11A, LGH 1202, Gothenburg,41703, Sweden

Ordering Information:
Quantity sales. Special discounts are available on quantity purchases by corporations, associations, and others. For details, contact the author at the address above.

First Print, 2019

ISBN: 9781798913031

Table of Contents

Introduction:

When Narendra Modi's Bharatiya Janata Party stormed India's general election victory in 2014, it was the first time a single party has won an absolute majority in the country since 1984. Without exception, commentators and analysts were sure that in "the world's largest democracy" a historic moment had just taken place. Wherever you looked for news about India, it was likely that reports and op-eds announcing "The Modi era begins," "Modi's moment," or a long-awaited "Change in India" would appear.

Today, Modi serves his fifth year in office and is already preparing to win the next general election in 2019. And yet, most of India's talk and news today is linked to heated, enthusiastic or inquiring considerations about its energetic prime minister. Like four years ago, Modi still catches the headlines when there is debate about India-both in India and abroad.

But this volume is not just about Narendra Modi, the man who promised to "reform, perform, transform" his country by boosting economic development and ultimately regaining India's place among the superpowers of the world. Instead, this book is about India in Modi's "age."

For several reasons, Modi's India is back on the global front stage. Since 2014, the Indian government has worked hard to carry out major economic and fiscal reforms, such as the recent Goods and Services Tax, or the bankruptcy law overhaul. "radical" measures have also been introduced to tackle corruption, such as sudden demonetization, which pulls 86 percent of India's cash out of circulation overnight. Modi himself has spent a great deal of effort promoting his "India brand" around the globe-most recently in Davos-and strengthening bilateral partnerships, while still defending a "globalization based on rules" against the threat of protectionism. Foreign investment in India has risen, and India's latest economic outlook for the IMF looks more optimistic than many would have thought: India will even overtake China this year with a 7.4 percent growth rate.

At the same time, an increase in communal tensions and concerns over Hindu nationalism continues to trigger debate in Asia and beyond. Minorities and human rights groups have questioned the true commitment of Modi to secularism, not only in India. They warn that intolerance is on the rise in India, motivated by the government's approval of militant Hindus ' excesses.

Is Modi's India really the dynamic, investor-friendly country he maintains worldwide marketing? Is he a reformer or a Hindu nationalist? What has India achieved so far? Is India's prime minister finally turning this "reluctant superpower" into a real global leader capable of competing with China?

All the answers to these questions remain controversial and even analysts are divided. More time is needed to provide a credible answer to some of these questions. What is certain, however, is that India's heavy weight can no longer be overlooked on the regional and global stage.

The European Union, first of all. The EU is a natural partner for India: Not only in terms of size and complexity, but also-and more importantly-on the basis of "the principles and values of democracy, freedom, the rule of law and respect for human rights," in the words of Modi and Italian Prime Minister Paolo Gentiloni at the recent summit. Indeed, India and Europe share good economic, trade and cultural relations, as well as common security interests, which are actually growing. It should also be recalled that the EU is India's number one trading partner, well ahead of China and the US, and steps have been taken towards strategic partnerships with India. However, a comprehensive European India strategy has not yet seen the light of day, although there is increasing evidence that such a quantum leap is urgently needed. At least before other international players take the opportunity, if only because India will soon become the most populous country in the world.

Secondly-as this is the point of view of ISPI-by Italy. India and Italy will celebrate 70 years of diplomatic relations this year. When these relations were established seven decades ago, both countries experienced a unique time in their respective national histories in a significant coincidence. Italy chose to become a republic less than two years earlier; its democratic constitution had just entered into force, and after twenty years of fascism, Italians were about to take part in their first general election. India, on the other hand, managed to free itself from colonial rule through non-violent struggle, and despite the hardships of partition and community violence, India's independent democracy quickly began, with all Indians ' proud and wholehearted commitment.

Both countries today are full-fledged democratic nations: Sometimes raucous, but with consolidated constitutional traditions and a global say. There are also strong political and economic ties between India and Italy and, as it were, "resilient": Their relations have not always been easy in recent years. The reasons for this are of public record, such as the prolonged tension over the detention of two Italian marines for the killing of two Indian fishermen. But both countries eventually dealt with their disagreements and errors as mature democracies do. Relationships are back on track. In a world that is increasingly uncertain and, alas, much more liquid than it was 70 years ago, the two countries will "work together to support an international system based on rules that upholds agreed international standards, global peace and stability, and supports inclusive growth and sustainable development in all parts of the interconnected world,". In the West, Italy was one of Sanskrit's "frontrunners," cultural and religious studies about India.

Today, however, it cannot be ignored that Italy is also home to Europe's second-largest Indian community, and that dozens of Italian and European companies have established (or would like to forge) strong economic and commercial ties with India. They all have a strong interest in assessing and better understanding this emerging regional and global leader's political and economic dynamics, internal challenges and international ambitions. The same applies to policymakers in Italy and Europe.

Understanding India has always been a challenge for observers, let alone explaining it, no matter how fascinating and thought-provoking this country is. Whether it is for its complexity, its diversity or the unique number of historical and cultural layers that shape its "plural" identity, it is essential to find a prism that allows an insight into India. As mentioned above, the "modi factor" is the prism we have chosen for this volume. There were demands for reforms that would lead to higher and possibly even double-digit growth when the Modi government came to power in 2014.

The Indian government has succeeded in pursuing a "new" generation of reforms in several areas-such as taxation, business regulations, corruption and bankruptcy-while failing to implement wholesale reforms in sensitive sectors such as labor or land acquisition, due to strong opposition at both parliamentary and state level. However, the government should concentrate even more urgently on developing the conditions for the proper functioning of market-based principles: In particular, support for job creation (one million Indians join the workforce each month), such as infrastructure, digitalization, housing and urban development, access to finance and human development.

If the implementation of enabling business and job creation conditions is a challenge for most countries, this applies in particular to India, whose federal structure and distribution of responsibilities across central and state governments makes it particularly difficult to implement far-reaching reforms and to hold any specific institution responsible for their progress. The book provides a detailed analysis of how the forces of centralization and decentralization have competed throughout the history of independent India to date, creating a continuous "circular tension between Delhi and the states through policy-making and implementation." Under Modi, the author s, the balance seems to reach a middle ground thanks to several continuous changes, each of which has been described in detail.

Since Modi was elected four years ago-and even earlier, when he became known as the chief minister who boosted the economy of Gujarat for more than a decade-analysts and commentators continue to ask whether the prime minister is more a reformer or a Hindu chauvinist. This question is at the heart of the book. The author builds on an examination of Modi's relationship with his power base (although a reformer, Modi was a life-long member of an influential Hindu nationalist grassroots organization, the RSS) and analyzes how the balance between competing claims from reform-minded supporters and religious extremists was a marker of Modi's political strategy, and with what consequences.

In switching to India's external relations, the book explores the peculiarities and challenges that affect India's place- and ambitions-as an emerging regional and potentially global power on the international stage. In particular, the author examines how India's relationship and competition with China, which is "an old partner and at the same time a consistent issue of concern," is a serious dilemma for the country: While India has long seen Beijing as a partner in demanding reformed global economic governance, there is nothing more than a similar growth path. But most importantly, India now feels that it must contain the ever-growing Chinese sphere of influence in Asia, which makes it difficult for India not only to conceptualize the BRICS as a still effective political entity for its own rise in world affairs, but also to manage the rise of China in this context. This is all the more true, the authors point out, at a time when China is positioning itself as the next world leader, and New Delhi is concerned about how China will transform into a global power, whether it will be accommodative or contentious about India's parallel rise, albeit much slower.

To be just to the questions raise above, it becomes inevitable to look back at where India was, where it is presently, the future of India as well as who are the contributors to the great transformation of India today.

To further discus the transformation India has recently experience in the 4-5 years administration of PM Narendra Modi, we will take a look at the brief background of India as well as operational systems within the country.

CHAPTER ONE

OVERVIEW OF INDIA'S HISTORICAL BACKGROUND

India's Independence

India has faced several invasions throughout history. While most invaders made their intentions clear from the start, the British succeeded in bringing India under their control through a business venture. Everything began with the British East India Company, which began as a mere joint-stock company, but slowly spread its wings and influence before the British government finally took control of the whole country.

In the early seventeenth century, the British company landed in India as traders, but began to interfere in Indian affairs around the 1750s. It began to transform from a trading company into a ruling force after the battle of Plassey (1757). When the British began to spread their tentacles over a large part of India, local resources and people began to be fully exploited.

The British were only concerned about strengthening their rule and power. The British rule had a detrimental effect on Indians ' social, economic, cultural and political life, which gradually forced common masses and rulers to revolt against the British rule. A number of agrarians, tribal and political rebellions broke out against foreign rule, but it was the 1857 rebellion that proved to be a launch pad for all subsequent fighting against British rule. By the end of the nineteenth century, the continuously increasing awareness, contact with the outside world, and the urge to free the motherland, led to an organized movement that uprooted British rule in 1947, which was 200 years old.

The History of British Colonialism in India

The British gained the support of many local rulers after the fall of the Mughal Empire by offering help against their adversaries. Since the British were equipped with enormous cannons and new war technology, many Indian rulers found their support helpful. The East India Company succeeded in setting up trading centers in places like Madras, Calcutta and Bombay in exchange for their support. The British began to extend their fortification gradually. When Siraj-ud-daulah, Bengal's Nawab, asked them to stop their extension, they defeated him in the Battle of Plassey (1757). In colonizing India as a whole, this win against Siraj-ud-daulah played a crucial role.

Early Rebellions Against the British Rule

Many Indian rulers supported British colonization in India for their short-term benefit, but many of them opposed the idea of foreign rule. This created a conflict between Indian rulers that the British used to their advantage. South Indian rulers, including Puli Thevar, Hyder Ali, Tipu Sultan, Pazhassi Raja, Rani Velu Nachiyar, Veerapandiya Kattabomman, Dheeran Chinnamalai, Maruthu Pandiyar, etc., were among the early rebellions. He rebelled against the British and fought many wars and battles.

Many rulers such as Hyder Ali and Dheeran Chinnamalai sought help from the rulers of Maratha in their fight against the British. Agitated by the British rule's negative impact on society's social, cultural, tribal and economic fabric, many people, such as Sidhu Murmu, Kanhu Murmu and Tilka Manjhi, stood up against British colonization.

Although the British succeeded in defeating bigger rulers such as Tipu Sultan through local alliances (supporting one ruler against the other), they had no difficulty in suppressing local agrarian and tribal rebellions. Not only did the British use better weapons, but they also used devious tactics such as "divide and rule" to consolidate their rule and power. Although the British tried their best to suppress rebellions throughout India, these rebellions would not stop because the British not only subjected people to a foreign rule, but also economically exploited people.

The Revolt of 1857

The revolt of 1857, often referred to as the "First War of Indian Independence," was the result of a series of incidents, but the immediate reason for the revolt was the issue of "greased cartridges." The East India Company mistreated Indian soldiers and discriminated against Indian and European soldiers. While the soldiers knew that the British used factors such as religion and caste, the news of the newly introduced Enfield P-53 rifles using cartridges made from fat extracted from beef and pork provoked a widespread rebellion against the British. Since the soldiers had to bite the cartridge to load the rifle, the Hindu and Muslim soldiers did not go well because they hurt their religious belief. Since beef and pork consumption is contrary to the religious beliefs of Hindus and Muslims, the allegation convinced Indian soldiers that the British tried to turn them into Christians.

This, together with many other factors, played a key role in the soldiers ' revolt. Many Indian rulers from various states followed suit and with the British locked horns. At the end of everything, at least 800,000 people were killed, including many civilians. The British government took control of India's administration from the East India Company as a result of the rebellion.

Organized Movements

The 1857 revolt was the first major rebellion against British rule and inspired the future generation to fight for the motherland's independence. Many organizations were slowly and gradually formed that began to demand some kind of self-governance and Indian rights. Dadabhai Naoroji founded the East India Association in 1867, while in 1876 Surendranath Banerjee founded the Indian National Association.

With more and more people demanding more rights, several prominent people came forward and decided to create a platform for self-rights and self-government. It led to the Indian National Congress being formed in 1885. Since the British failed to grant even the moderate demands of the Congress, many Indians began to question the moderate leaders of the Congress and advocated a more radical approach to the British, which resulted in several revolutionary organizations advocating the use of force and violence.

The work of socio-religious groups such as Brahmo Samaj and Arya Samaj played a crucial role in raising Indian awareness. Reformers such as Swami Vivekananda, Rabindranath Tagore, V. O. Chidambaram Pillai and Subramanya Bharathy evoked a sense of Indian nationalism.

The Rise of Nationalism

Radical leaders such as Bal Gangadhar Tilak immediately pushed for Indians to rule themselves. Tilak was also saddened by the fact that the British government's education system did not positively portray India's history and culture. He advocated complete freedom (Swaraj) and inspired many Indians with his famous slogan, "Swaraj is my birthright and I will have it." He was joined by other leaders like Bipin Chandra Pal and Lala Lajpat Rai. The trio together came to be known as' Lal-Bal-Pal,' but for advocating violence and disorder they were expelled from Congress. They did enough, however, to instill nationalism in the minds of thousands of Indians.

The Partition of Bengal

Since Bengal's pre-independent geography was as large as France, the then Viceroy and Governor-General, Lord Curzon, ordered Bengal's partition in 1905. He said the partition would lead to better administration and ease the Hindus-Muslims conflict.

However, the Indian nationalists believed the move to slow down the momentum gathered by the recent nationalist movements. They also believed that Lord Curzon used the policy of division and rule to create a divide between Hindus and Muslims. This led to a major protest against the British rule, including the boycott of British products and the publication of several rebellious newspapers and articles. Eventually, in 1911, the government was forced to reunite Bengal. But a new partition was created shortly afterwards, based on the languages spoken. Bengal's partition left an indelible mark on Bengal's people and political scenario.

The Rise of the Muslim League

In 1886, the All India Muhammadan Educational Conference was founded by Islamic reformist and philosopher Syed Ahmed Khan. The conference was set up to provide Indian Muslims with quality education. The conference organized annual meetings to discuss, among other things, different ways of improving the quality of education. In 1906, the members decided to set up a political party called the "All India Muslim League" during the 20th session of the conference. After the creation of the All India Muslim League, the party sought to achieve equal civil rights for the Muslim population in India. The Muslim League began to slowly and gradually propagate the theory that the Indian National Congress was a pro-Hindu outfit and that the political party was unable to guarantee the Muslim community in India equal rights. This belief found many takers, and Muslim leaders slowly and gradually began to contemplate the idea of creating another political entity in which Muslims formed the majority.

National Movement & the First World War

At the end of the nineteenth century, the national movement began to pick up and gather a critical mass by the turn of the new century, which would further propel it in the coming years. More and more people joined hands with nationalist leaders and Congress to raise self-government demands. Leaders such as Lala Lajpat Rai, Bal Gangadhar Tilak, Bipin Chandra Pal and V. O. Chidambaram Pillai began to protest the British government more and more.

Although the Indian National Congress still advocated the importance of British rule, people began to take part in mass movements, which also inspired others. Meanwhile, the British government promised India special benefits in exchange for its support during the First World War just before the beginning of the First World War. In the First World War, as many as 1.3 million Indian soldiers were sent to places such as the Middle East, Europe and Africa to fight for the British. Many individual rulers from various princely states also supported the British by sending large amounts of money, food and munitions.

The Arrival of Mahatma Gandhi

In South Africa, where he worked as a barrister, Gandhi mastered the methods of civil disobedience by non-violent means. Thanks to non-violent protests by Gandhi, many political prisoners were released by General Jan Smuts in 1914. A prominent Indian National Congress leader, Gopal Krishna Gokhale, impressed by his methods, asked Gandhi to return to India and join the national movement. Gandhi joined the Indian National Congress when he arrived and accepted Gopal Krishna Gokhale as his mentor. He then established the Satyagraha ashram and in 1917 led a campaign for Satyagraha. Gandhiji led many non-violent protests, including Satyagraha and fasting, for the next three years. The Kheda Satyagraha and the Champaran satyagraha were some of the early movements in which he used Satygraha's concept to fight for farmers ' rights and other farmers.

The Non-Cooperation Movement

Brigadier-General Reginald Dyer ordered in 1919 to shoot at a peaceful assembly of men, women and children in Jallianwala Bagh, who had gathered to celebrate Baisakhi and condemn the arrest of Dr Saifuddin Kitchlew and Satya Pal. This British inhuman act sent shockwaves throughout India and received strong criticism and protests throughout India. Mahatma Gandhi also denounced and strongly condemned this cowardly behavior.

The national movement was slowly building up and the Jallianwalah Bagh incident played an important role in the beginning of the "non-cooperation movement." He asked other political and religious leaders to support him and called on the Indians to stop using British products.

Gandhiji called for Khadi to be used over British textiles. He also asked officials to leave their jobs and return the British titles and honors. Many Indians refused to pay taxes and many teachers and lawyers abandoned their professions. The non-cooperation movement became an enormous success throughout India until Gandhiji called it off following the Chauri Chaura incident, in which three civilians and 22 police officers were killed.

The movement for non-cooperation witnessed an unprecedented and large-scale involvement of people from all regions and status. The whole country was transformed into a different area and the protests were largely successful, but the unfortunate incident in Chauri Chaura forced Gandhi to dismiss the movement. He said people were not yet ready for such mass movements. Many were disappointed by the decision to call off the non-cooperation movement and criticized by several leaders.

Revolutionary Movement & its Role in Freedom Movement

Although the Indian National Congress, led by leaders such as Gopal Krishna Gokhale and Mahatma Gandhi, advocated civil disobedience and non-violent protests, many firebrand leaders believed in the use of force to overthrow the British. The revolutionary movement began in the late 1750s, but it began to take shape during the partition of Bengal. Many revolutionaries began to collect arms and explosives under Barin Ghosh's leadership. They even started producing bombs and some were sent to foreign countries to learn about bombing and other military training.

By 1924, revolutionaries such as Chandrashekhar Azad, Bhagat Singh, Ashfaqullah Khan, Ramprasad Bismil, Shivaram Rajguru, Surya Sen, etc. were formed by the Hindustan Republican Association (HRA). Began to engage in different revolutionary activities. Some of the famous revolutionary activities include the conspiracy of Alipore bombers, the armored raid of Chittagong, the robbery of Kakori trains, the conspiracy case of Delhi-Lahore, etc.

Azand Hind Fauz

Subhas Chandra Bose left the Indian National Congress and traveled to many countries to seek assistance for the independence of India. To fight the British, Bose wanted to raise an Indian army. He went to Japan on the basis of Hitler's advice and formed the Indian National Army (Azad Hind Government). The Indian National Army managed to capture the islands of Andaman and Nicobar with the help of the Japanese army during the Second World War. However, the reversal to Japan in the Second World War also affected the INA's prospects, and the border blocked its march and many soldiers and officers were arrested.

Quit India Movement

Mahatma Gandhi intensified his protests for India's complete independence as the Second World War progressed. He drew up a resolution calling on the British to leave India. The "Quit India Movement" or "Bharat Chhodo Andolan" was the Indian National Congress ' most aggressive movement. Gandhi was arrested on 9 August 1942 and held in Aga Khan Palace in Pune for two years. By the end of 1943, the Quit India Movement came to an end when the British suggested that full power would be transferred to the people of India. Gandhi called off the movement that led to 100,000 political prisoners being released.

Partition & Independence of India

Although prominent leaders such as Mahatma Gandhi and Jawaharlal Nehru were unwilling to accept the religious partition formula, communal clashes between religious groups accelerated Pakistan's creation. The Congress accepted the proposal for the independence cum partition offered by the British Cabinet Mission in 1946. Sardar Patel convinced Gandhi that this was the only way to avoid civil war and the Mahatma gave his consent reluctantly. The British Parliament adopted the famous Indian Independence Act of 1947, and Pakistan was declared a free nation on August 14. A few minutes later at 12:02, India became a democratic nation, much to the joy and relief of the whole subcontinent of India.

Gandhiji focused on peace and unity among Hindus and Muslims after India's independence. He began a fast-to-death in Delhi, demanding that all community violence be stopped, and that Pakistan be paid Rs. 55 crores in accordance with the Partition Council Agreement. All political leaders ultimately agreed to his wishes. It was the responsibility of the Constituent Assembly to create the constitution. The constitution was adopted on 26 November 1949 under the leadership of Dr. B.R. Ambedkar. India's Constitution entered into force on 26 January 1950.

Indian Democracy, A Historical Perspective – Then and Now

The civilization of India is one of the world's oldest. Democracy as a form of government is not a notion foreign to India, as is popularly believed, nor should it be regarded merely as a British legacy. A look at India's ancient history reveals that there were democratic republics in India before the 6th century BC. In fact, some historians have recognized Vaishali (now in the Indian state of Bihar) as the first republic in the world.

In ancient India, even during the Rig-Veda period, one of the earliest instances of democratic civilizations was found, probably the earliest Indo-European literature and one of the Hindus ' most sacred books. The states mentioned are mostly monarchies, but the Sabha and the Samiti are two democratic institutions. The Sabha (literally "assembly" in Sanskrit) is widely interpreted as the assembly of the elect or the important chieftains of the tribe, while the Samiti appears to be the assembly of all the men of the tribe, only for very special occasions. The Sabha and the Samiti checked the king's powers and in the Rigveda they were given a semi-divine status as the "daughters of the Hindu deity Prajapati." The later epic Ramayana seems to mention a Samiti summoned as the successor to his son Prince Ramachandra by King Dasharatha of Ayodhya for ratification. Before the birth of Gautama Buddha in the sixth century, many more republics were established in ancient India. These republics were known as Maha Janapadas, and Vaishali (now Bihar, India) was the first republic in the world among these states. In some of these republics, the democratic Sangha, Gana and Panchayat systems have been used; the Panchayat system is still used in Indian villages today. Later in the 4th century BC, during the time of Alexander the Great, the Greeks wrote about the states of Sabarcae and Sambastai in what is now Pakistan and Afghanistan, whose "form of government was democratic and not royal," according to Greek scholars of that time. Another example was the democratic election in Bengal that documented Tibetan historian Taranath's rise to power by Gopala.

Dr. Sarvapalli Radhakrishnan, an eminent philosopher, educator and the illustrious second President of India, reiterated this point in the Constituent Assembly on 20 January 1947 when he said, "We can't say that the Republican tradition is foreign to this country's genius. From the beginning of Indian history, they had it. When a couple of merchants from the north went down to the south, one of the Deccan princes asked, "Who is your king? The answer was,' Some of us are governed by assemblies, some of us kings.'-' Kecid deso ganadhina kecid rajadhina ' Panini, Megasthenes and Kautilya refer to ancient India's republics. The Great Buddha belonged to the Kapilavastu Republic.

The ancient religious texts of India, the Vedas, teach us the principles of respect for human dignity, love for all living beings, respect for all religions and justice for everyone. Thiruvalluvar, a galaxy of saints such as Baba Sheik Farid, Hazrat Nizamuddin Aulia, Guru Nanak, Kabir and Baba Bulle Shah, also laid down a human tradition and emphasized the unity of all human beings, irrespective of caste, creed and religious belief. They achieved what powerful generals could not achieve with the sword and gun with their message of brotherhood, tolerance and universal love. Indian scriptures such as Ramayana and Mahabharata have imbibed the principle of righteousness in us and instructed us to fight evil. The country's love and patriotism are also part of their ethos.

Akbar's son, Jehangir, is said to have installed a bell in his palace and anyone, regardless of religion, belief or social status, could ring the bell by the chain at any time and have their grievances rectified. This tolerance and secularism tradition continued more or less undisturbed until Aurangzeb's ascent to the throne. A despotic and tyrannical ruler, Aurangzeb was a religious fanatic who propagated Islam vigorously and adopted a policy of vigorous conversion. The last prominent Mughal ruler was Aurangzeb, and the dynasty declined after him. The last Mughal king, who was deposed by the British and exiled in Burma, Bahadur Shah' Zafar' took poetry in his final days.

The era of the British East India Company came after the Mughals ' age, and eventually India became the British Empire's' crown jewel.'

Fighting for freedom is a natural instinct in man, and the main ingredients are rebellion against tyranny, courage, righteous anger and sacrifice. Some of Indian great freedom fighters forcibly resisted the rule of the British empire and so tried to achieve freedom. Subhash Chandra

Bose was the most prominent among them. Revolutionaries of firebrands such as Bhagat Singh, Rajguru, Ram Prasad "Bismil," Sukhdev and Chandrashekhar Azad, along with thousands of other unnamed young people, also showed their courage and sacrificed their lives for the country. However, Mahatma Gandhi, who believed in the principles of non-violence, satyagraha and civil disobedience, led the mass movement for freedom. Lokmanya Tilak, known as the father of Indian unrest, informed the people of their rights and gave them the moral courage to exercise their rights. His request for Swaraj as his birthright was finally adopted by an Indian National Congress resolution at its Lahore session under Pt's presidency. Nehru Jawaharlal in 1929. It would not be wrong to say that Tilak laid the basis on which Mahatma Gandhi built the independence movement building. Prominent leaders from all regions, irrespective of their religion, caste, faith and all walks of life, followed the footsteps of Gandhiji in the fight for freedom. They suffered endless hardships in the process, even facing the deprivation of stinking prison cells, and made sacrifices that could move the heart of the most stubborn tyrants and despots. The nation is indebted, would be indebted and should instead remain indebted to them. The courage, will and conviction with which they fought should be the inspiring ideals for Indians and these principles for governance should be kept in mind.

Mahatma Gandhi's struggle for freedom was not merely an independence from foreign rule, but a relentless crusade against colonial subjugation and all forms of exploitation throughout the world. The Indian nationalists inspired many nationalist movements in Asia and Africa and established a strong relationship with the peoples of other countries struggling for self-government. A number of states achieved freedom shortly after India became independent and links to pre-independence have flourished into lasting relations. India eventually achieved independence, but was fractured on religious grounds by the horror of partition.

The Muslim League led by Mohammad Ali Jinnah, who was previously a member of the Indian National Congress, with the ulterior motive of having a separate nation for Muslims, took an obstructionist attitude and did not participate in the meetings of the Constituent Assembly, which was elected to establish a free India constitution. The demand for Pakistan was based on the theory that two separate nations were Hindus and Muslims. Jinnah is famously supposed to have said: "The Hindus and the Muslims belong to two different religions, philosophies, social customs and literature... to join two such nations under one state, one as a numerical minority and the other as a majority, must lead to growing discontent and ultimate destruction of any fabric so constructed for the government of that state."

In the end, India's heart was divided. New borders, where none existed before, were drawn by the proponents and instigators of partition on the basis of religion, with subsequent motives, certainly not only for the benefit of Muslims. Should a nation and its unity be based on religion? Was it wise for the Muslim League to invent a religion-based two-nation theory? It is still a question mark whether they were entitled to do so and the recognition and acceptance of that right. This nation belonged to Hindus and Muslims, Sikhs and Christians and belongs to all religions, religions and castes. Everyone was Indian. The irrational and drastic desire to have a separate state of Pakistan on the basis of religion, overwhelmed even poets such as Allama Iqbal, who once wrote "Saare jahaan se accha, Hindostan hamara, hum bulbulein hain iski, yeh Gulistan hamara" -"Our India is the largest nation in the world, we are the bulbul birds in this nation's garden," but later became an acclaimed advocate of a separate statistic.

Mohammad Ali Jinnah was a great leader and human being and originally conceived Pakistan on the basis of the beloved principle of secularism. Pakistan later became an Islamic state. Therefore, the spirit of democracy has always existed through the ages in India. However, India's present form of parliamentary democracy is partly a British heritage and partly the result of the genius and foresight of the Constitution's founding fathers. India's growing national awareness and administrative expediency led the British government to introduce a democratic and representative form of government in modern India through a series of "Government of India Acts." These Acts initially established the post of Governor General in India and subsequently established provincial legislative councils, which developed into democratic and representative bodies. India's Constitution has adopted a number of important features of the 1935 Government of India Act, and the system of government established by the British undoubtedly laid the foundation for the system we now have. Even so, while India's democracy has survived and even flourished since independence, neighboring nations such as Pakistan and Bangladesh, which were British co-heritors of the same legacy, have also failed. This historical fact underlines the belief that democracy is inherent in their ethos and culture as a way of life.

India's freedom is a unique marvel of modern history, achieved by non-violent struggle. The independence movement was not only a fight for independence, but also a movement for the countrymen's social and economic liberation. The social, political and economic challenges that the national leaders faced during the struggle for freedom made their task even more difficult and important. It is a collective good fortune that we had national leaders of great caliber and integrity, distinguished scholars, statesmen and visionaries with a deep understanding of India, who could shape the nation's course towards a glorious future. They have left us a constitution that enshrines the ethos and essence of democracy, freedom and brotherhood and is a true beacon for illuminating the path and guiding the steps.

The electoral mechanism established by the Constitution has ensured that India has a genuine and vibrant democracy through free and fair elections, which ensure a smooth transfer of power from one government to another. The multi-party system we have today is partly the result of the political system and partly the result of a process of continuous development since independence and indicates the vibrancy of democracy.

In the first sixty years of India's independence, democracy stood the test of time. Over the years, we have seen its evolution from a single party, the Indian National Congress, to a multi-party democracy, dominated by both the center and the states. National parties such as the Bharatiya Janata Party and the Communist Parties are now jostling for space with several regional and state-level parties, along with the Indian National Congress at the centre. The articulation of regional aspirations led to the emergence of several regional parties in states such as the Jammu and Kashmir National Conference, the Telugu Desam Party in Andhra Pradesh, the DMK and AIADMK in Tamil Nadu, the Shiromani Akali Dal in Punjab, the Asom Gana Parishad in Assam and many others. With an increasing number of representatives of these parties in Parliament, their influence in the Center has increased steadily, and this is evident from the fact that most governments have been coalitions since the early 1990s, in which the support of regional parties is an absolute sine qua non. There have been two points of view on this phenomenon; while some say that the regional parties represent the aspirations of the people of those regions, others believe that the proliferation of political parties on the basis of considerations such as regionalism, caste and religion has fragmented and divided the electorate, resulting in a hanging parliament after each election and requiring coalition governments at the centre, which cause political instability.

In recent decades, the rise of political parties based on religious and caste-related reasons has also been an important feature of democracy. The Bharatiya Janata Party (BJP), which is ideologically based on the concept of Hindutva, grew from an insignificant two-seat party in the Lok Sabha in 1984 to become the largest single party in the lower house in the 1996, 1998 and 1999 general elections, in which the BJP, together with numerous coalition partners, each time under the leadership of the BJP, staked its claim to form the government. The government of the National Democratic Alliance (NDA), led by the BJP and its allies in 1999, successfully completed its full term. However, the NDA lost the general election in 2004, with the BJP ceding to the Indian National Congress as the largest single party. Under the United Progressive Alliance, the INC eventually formed the government with its allies in 2004 with Dr. Manmohan Singh as Prime Minister. After winning the 2009 general election, the UPA with some exclusions and inclusions once again formed the government at the centre.

The Bahujan Samajwadi Party and the Republican Party of India, based on the caste plane, have also recorded phenomenal growth and are represented in the House of the People in large numbers. Parties such as the Rashtriya Janata Dal (RJD) and the Samajwadi Party (SP), although not openly caste, are in fact heavily dependent on the caste factor for their election success. There has therefore appeared to be a gradual shift in the nature of democracy, where issues based on ideals such as regionalism, linguism, religion and caste have become significant factors as opposed to broad nationalism. Today's challenge is to maintain the balance between people's aspirations for these issues and the unity, integrity and spirit of the nation and its democracy.

Democracy has also faced other challenges, whether in the form of a war with neighbors Pakistan and China, or in situations such as the national emergency declared between 1975 and 1977, but the people's will has always triumphed, manifesting the spirit of democracy.

Most of the leaders who led the regional parties were members of the Indian National Congress at one time or another. Their break-away decision may have been partially ideological, but it was more likely to achieve power. They were one, and even those parties broke away again. We have a federal structure, but we have a strong center and the states felt that due to the inadequate sharing of central support, the aspirations and expectations of different states were not fulfilled by the center in their perception, so they had different flags, regardless of some basic and fundamental principles. For example, the BSP, a Dalit party, has given Brahmin candidates a large proportion of its tickets in recent UP elections. Not only those who believe in a particular religion can be called fundamentalists or fanatics, but the people of a particular caste can be more fanatical than those who believe in a particular religion. After winning the election, they become the benefactors of only that caste on the basis of the majority of a particular caste, even ignoring their supporters who may belong to various castes. They mostly turn a blind eye to the section of people they presume have not voted for, which leads to people's frustration and encourages in their minds a lack of trust and appreciation in politicians.

Although regional parties advocate different ideologies, mostly beating the drum for a specific caste or religion or interest group, their ultimate goal is to achieve power by all means, and some fair principles of democracy and politics are compromised. Ideological struggle does not necessarily have to be a source of tension, conflict or conflict. It can also promote new views, attitudes and solutions. Everything depends on whether two sides choose reason or fancy. The search for mutually acceptable solutions or confrontation for survival, the search for reasonable compromises or the imposition of opinions by force leading to organized demonstrations, bandhs and the encouragement of violence cannot solve the situation. Fair demonstrations, wisdom and willingness to reconcile and compromise can sometimes hold well. Ideology is in fact a long-term strategy for the life of society. We are in the 21st century, and we have gained independence for more than six decades, and it is bound to preserve some elements of faith in the age of the free world. It can no longer be just religion or caste-our views, aspirations and ambitions must be in line with national and international realities, using scientific methods to analyze and identify targets and suggest rational and moral ways of achieving them. This understanding of ideology and its role in politics or life in general or on either side is not inherently unacceptable. The different political parties do not need to abandon their ideologies or sacrifice any universal human or specific values. The only thing that needs to be done is to adopt civilized means to resolve ideological disputes and differences that have long been the rule in most democratic nations, both in the

West and in the East. We can and should strike a balance between conflicting ideologies in order to achieve the ultimate goal of the country's progress and the well-being of every citizen.

Today's situation in India is very worrying. Political parties do not seem to care about the candidate's criminal antecedents when distributing tickets for elections in the state or for parliament. Instead, tickets are given to people who have the support of a particular caste or religion that prevails in that constituency, without taking into account whether the candidate is an honest prominent person, a social worker or a human being who will take care of his constituents after being elected. They distribute tickets even to known criminals with criminal cases registered against them for the sake of winning elections. This is a pathetic situation, and nobody can understand where we are going. The main goal these days is to win elections by disregarding all the principles of parliamentary democracy. The growing influence of lobbyists is also a disturbing feature in Indian politics. Powerful corporate and commercial interests such as the industrial lobby, the sugar lobby, the banking lobby, among others, have a profound influence on policy and government issues, and the government often succumbs to pressure and takes decisions that satisfy these interest groups, but are not in the best interests of the people and the nation. One of the latest such cases is the steep rise in food grain prices in

2009-2010. It is inexplicable how the silos flooded with stocks of food grains, the market overflowed with food grains, and their prices challenged all economics for an extremely long period of time.

Configuration and cluster -a cocktail of various parties leading to multiplicity will ultimately adversely affect the functioning of democracy. Parties are called' national parties,' but their main foundations are actuality, confined to specific states. There are parties that have repeatedly changed their names; they are mostly separate groups, leading to the mushrooming of divided political bodies in the country and creating a state of confusion in the electorate's minds. In the States and in Parliament, we have more than 40 parties. To some extent, the system has resisted the proliferation of political parties, but it must ultimately affect the basic building.

The possibility of hung parliaments and hung assemblies creates logical difficulties for the President and the Governors, as well as for the speakers and presidents of the Chambers. It also makes it difficult for the leader who is the Prime Minister or the Chief Minister to govern, as well as to keep the flock together at the same time, most of whom, as they saw while sitting in the same boat, pulled the oars in different directions. If we are to have a truly strong and stable democratic building, this situation must change.

CHAPTER TWO

HISTORICAL TRANSFORMATION OF INDIA

India is a country with a long-standing democratic tradition in which, apart from some conflict zones, the state monopoly on the use of force is guaranteed and in which national identification is unquestioned by relevant actors. The country can boast an almost continuous record of free and fair elections, frequent and peaceful transfers of power and strict civil supremacy over the military. Freedom of association and opinion is guaranteed

The horizontal division of powers (especially the independence of the judiciary) is guaranteed; the vertical division of powers is subject to the frequent destabilization of state governments by interested political actors. The slow operation of the courts and the massive accumulation of unfinished litigation hamper justice. There are also deficits in law enforcement, police neutrality and the protection of civil rights in areas subject to tension. Heavily fragmented, weakly institutionalized and unstable political parties. There are many associations, but they are rather weak, while social movements have become visible and assertive.

India is still a low-income country in economic terms. The country became a full-fledged market economy after 1991, with very few restrictions on local and foreign businesses.

However, the country is still protected by high tariff barriers from foreign competition. Internal reservations for the small business sector, the existence of state banks and state-owned enterprises (only unwillingly privatized), agricultural regulation, massive infrastructural deficits and overly detailed and protective work, land and insolvency still undermine competition and economic dynamism. The economy is booming, inflation is moderate, exports are booming and the balance of payments and debt situation is comfortable, despite this unfinished agenda. The budget deficit is still massive, however, to some extent crowding out private investment. The social and ecological sustainability of Indian development is still not guaranteed, since absolute poverty, social exclusion and ecological degradation are still severe and only partially managed by the government.

There are moderate difficulties in developing a market democracy. In Hindu radicals or leftist coalition partners, there are some problems for the government to rein, but the government's steering capacity has proved adequate. The resources available have not always been used wisely: Untarget subsidies abound, welfare spending is far too low and corruption is still widespread. The government cultivates and is therefore limited to an attitude of utmost national autonomy and international cooperation.

India won freedom mainly by a sustained, non-violent struggle involving the sacrifice of thousands of people, mainly under Tilak, Gandhi, Nehru and Bose. On 15 August 1947, India became a free country. India was divided and a new nation was created -Pakistan. For its development and progress, India has taken a democratic-socialist path. On 26 January 1950, it adopted a new Constitution.

The Constitution guarantees the citizens of India fundamental rights, ensuring equality, freedom and justice. In addition to fundamental rights, the Constitution also sets out state policy directives in order to provide a desired direction for social and economic change in India.

Equality before Law:

There's' rule of law' in India today. All citizens are equal and subject to the same authority's jurisdiction. Even in the late sixties, the private purses granted to the princes and feudal lords were abolished. The basis for recognizing status and power is no longer birth. The provision of social honor and privileges is no longer considered by religion, language, caste or ethnicity.

However, the weaker sections of Indian society, in particular the Scheduled Castes (scs), the Scheduled Tribes (sts) and Other Backward Classes (obcs), have been provided with special facilities and provisions for their upliftment. The dominant sections of Indian society protect them from discrimination and exploitation.

Women are equal to men. At all levels of political system, all Indian citizens have the right to vote.

Progress in Education:

In education, tremendous progress has been made. Over 100 million children receive primary education. The increase in secondary level numbers is also impressive. Education at university and college levels has also increased dramatically. There are approximately 300 universities in India today. India's government has also taken up the diversification of education at senior school, college and university levels.

Basic education is provided at the basic level. Today, at the level of senior schools and universities, emphasis is placed on vocationalization, computer studies, applied science, management and other relevant and profitable fields of knowledge in order to address the problem of unemployment among educated young men and women.

In 1986, India's government implemented a new education policy that placed greater emphasis on the quality of education, especially at school level. The education of scs and sts, women and back sections has been given special attention. Education has encouraged people to migrate from villages to cities. Hindi and other national languages are increasingly emphasized. The three-language learning policy at school level has been implemented in all India's Union states.

National Consolidation:

In 1955, India's states were reorganized on the basis of the recommendations of the reorganization Commission of the States. Each state has some cultural cohesion since this was done on the basis of the language spoken by the people. India was characterized by the unique feudalism that treated rajas, thikanedars, jagirdars and zamindars as Mai-Bap (parents). First, the government abolished such patri, monotonous feudalism and then abolished the private purses and compensation granted to the rajas.

This was really a' revolutionary' step, as ownership rights were granted to the tenants. Zamindars ' institution as intermediaries was removed with a pen stroke. The consolidation of small landholdings and ceilings on maximum land tenure was later adopted as land reform measures. Thanks to these reforms and the adoption of new technology, fertilizers and seeds in agriculture, the Green Revolution was made possible. India is now self-sufficient in food grains, while it depended on the United States of America and some other countries in the 1950s and early 1960s for its food grain requirement.

Five-Year Plans and Socio-Economic Changes:

India has also made a lot of progress in the industry since independence. Heavy industries were established in the fifties and sixties in Hatia, Rourkela, Bokaro, Sindri, Bangalore and elsewhere. The government has also received attention from small-scale and cottage industries. Industrialization was possible because India took the path of planned economic development and social change. The planning task was assigned to India's Planning Commission. The government has adopted its "mixed economy" policy, which is a policy of balanced growth in the private, public and joint sectors.

The Community Development Program (CDP) was launched on 2 October 1952 in order to raise the rural population. The Panchayati Raj scheme was introduced on 2 October 1959, initially in the states of Rajasthan and Andhra Pradesh, in order to overcome some of the impediments in the implementation of these schemes. In view of the "feeling needs" of the rural classes, the elected leaders of the rural population at three levels, namely the village, the block and the district, were given the responsibility of implementing development schemes.

Several schemes have been implemented for the well-being of urban people and industry workers. The Panchayati Raj Institutions (pris) now enjoy statutory status, such as the legislatures and Lok Sabha, on the basis of the provisions of the Constitution; the 1993 amendment.

Social Legislations and Progress:

The British enacted social laws, in particular to prevent child marriages, sati, infanticide, and widow remarriages, etc. India's government passed in 1955 the Hindu Marriage Act and in 1956 the Hindu Succession Act. Legislation has also been implemented to discourage child labor. There are now strict laws against the dowry institution. Untouchability is a criminal offense, according to India's Constitution. The legislation to give wage earners fair wages and eliminate intermediaries and the Zamindari institution has helped poor workers in towns and villages to earn minimum wages.

Despite these healthy developments in the post-independence period, the concentration of economic power has increased in the hands of a few families and individuals. The poor still don't get their share. Their living conditions are terrible. The poor are still victims of the rich upper caste and class landlords' dictates today. Dowry, especially in towns, is still a serious evil. There is still a lack of social awareness of these problems.

In elections, religion, ethnicity and caste are important factors. There's a lot of reliance on caste members to win an election. Factional disputes stem from caste, religion and community-based alliances. These problems are not free even urban and educated people.

History and characteristics of transformation

There have been very different times of economic and political transformation in India. Autonomy and democratization preceded decades of economic liberalization. The colonial constitution introduced democratic participation in 1935, largely copied by the independent Indian constitution. Since then, there has been uninterrupted democratic continuity, with the exception of two years of the emergency regime from 1975 to 1977. Until 1967, the Congress Party dominated at central and state levels, making government changes almost impossible. The party system subsequently became more and more pluralized and changes in government (first at the state, later at the central level) frequently occurred. This was accompanied by increasing mobilization and the articulation of new, lower caste groups, a strong expression of regional, linguistic and religious identities, and thus also by rising levels of internal conflict. Traditional civil society by state and party agencies remained underdeveloped and colonized. However, in the last two decades (1980s and 1990s), new social movements have flourished. Because of the country's intense political mobilization and the fact that only elections give leaders legitimacy, India must be regarded as a consolidated democracy, although civil rights and federal establishment have often been overruled.

The transformation of India into a fully-fledged market economy is recent. The country has been following the path of import substitution and state-led industrialization for decades, leaving considerable room for private companies as the state's junior partners. The first hesitant liberalization came into force in 1985, which resulted in the deregulation of the internal market and the high-tech sector; the severe balance of payments crisis in the period 1990 to 1991 led to a complete market-friendly turnaround, which forced the country to reach an agreement with the IMF. India became an open market economy with very few sectors restricted to private and foreign businesses with the subsequent reforms. However, comparatively high tariffs and frequent use of anti-dumping measures still protect the economy from foreign competition. Internally, small business reservations and the only partial liberalization of agriculture act to restrict competition.

Assessment:

Democracy

India has been a fully consolidated, inclusive democracy for decades, without a political process legitimizing veto player. However, in areas prone to tension, there are deficits in law enforcement, police neutrality and the protection of civil rights.

Stateness

There are practically no stateness problems in India. Apart from some rural conflict zones in central India, separatist areas in Kashmir and some small states in Northeast India, the state monopoly on the use of force is almost complete. There are no real problems in identifying with the nation and defining nationality. Only a few divided groups in separatist zones do not consider themselves Indian citizens. The country's secularist credentials suffered somewhat under the rule of the Hindu nationalist Bharatiya Janata Party (BJP), which had to moderate its position in order to maintain the alliance and expand its electoral base. Following the Congress Party's takeover in 2004, there was a return to more or less undiluted secularism. The country inherited an efficient colonial government administration with merit-based recruitment and promotion. This heritage was maintained at the central level to a large extent. Politization and recruitment according to excessive reserve quota (along caste lines) became more common in the administration of the union territories. Indian police are highly inefficient, politically dependent and corrupt. The conviction rate of criminals is therefore low, police atrocities against civilians are common and the government must rely on the army to mitigate internal disturbances.

Political participation

Since independence, India can boast an almost uninterrupted record of free, fair and more or less non-violent elections, accompanied by increased voter turnout (especially among the poorer and least developed groups of the population) and frequent and peaceful transfer of power. Even in conflict-ridden union territories (e.g. Kashmir), elections have had a de-escalating effect. The military has never acted as a veto power; it is under strict civil control and has a purely professional role to play. Freedom of association is guaranteed, it is legally easy to form interest groups. Most of them are only poorly institutionalized, fragmented, hardly democratic internally and often not really independent. In this respect, recent social movements are different.

Rule of law

Horizontal power separation is ensured; vertical separation has often been overturned by replacements or undermining state governments that are politically motivated. Parliament's control of the executive is affected by the modest professional competence of parliamentarians and the lack of scientific support. The Supreme Court has considerable and wide-ranging competence in the examination of constitutional correctness of laws and as an appeal body in respect of human rights violations. In recent years, the court has become quite proactive and has not abstained from harsh criticism of government neglect. The same applies to the independent Election Commission, which closely monitored the maintenance of the stipulated electoral codes.

Despite pressure from the executive, the courts remained institutionally autonomous, interfering in the appointment and transfer of politically unpopular judges. The slow functioning of justice restricts the rule of law, leading to a massive accumulation of unfinished litigation. This was also due to low process initiation and extension thresholds, excessively detailed laws and regulations, etc. Underprivileged sections of the population are shy of the costs of litigation in the courts. Public office misuse is frequent in India and only punished intermittently (although more than before). This has to do with the recent decline in over-regulation of the economy. The culture of corruption in India is deeply rooted. India is therefore listed at the top of several international corruption and malpractice rankings. Spectacular cases involving parts of the whole political class led to a slow reorientation, mainly due to judicial activism.

Stability of democratic institutions

Democratic institutions in India are more or less stable, leaving out the frequent destabilization of state governments (for political purposes), the shaky character of multi-party governments in the last decade (which gave political blackmail to even minor parties), combined with the endemic defection of parliamentarians to the opposition or new parties in order to benefit from the new political equation. This also delayed important projects for constitutional and economic reform. A new anti-defection law (2004) seeks to curb defections by restricting rebels ' premiums. The over-regulation of the economy, the proliferation of ministries and government agencies and the already mentioned congestion of the judicial system also hamper institutional efficiency. However, all political parties (including extremists) and social groups accept and nurture democratic institutions. The people also question their legitimacy.

Political and social integration

The Indian party system is stable, the parties themselves are only weakly institutionalized and, despite defective measures, party discipline is low. Informal procedures, "clientelism" and identity politics often replace formal organizational structure. The Communist Parties and the BJP represent an exception to this pattern with their disciplined frontal organizations. The Congress Party has largely been de-institutionalized. Millions of people belong to associations in India, but interest groups are rather weak, fragmented across ideological and party lines and often fight each other rather than their opponents. This is also why labor relations are susceptible to conflict. Due to the state's long-standing dominant economic role, labor unions and federations of employers are only partially autonomous. Economic liberalisation, new professional associations have emerged. Social movements (e.g. women's rights, environmental rights, human rights, etc.) have become more visible and assertive. These movements are dominated by middle class members. The lack of links between the population and interest groups is compensated to some extent by direct links between parties and social groups.

Market economy

India has seen its economic order undergo a far-reaching, rapid and successful transformation since 1991. In the area of privatization, the dismantling of subsidies, the creation of a market-friendly labor, land and insolvency regime and the reduction of the massive public deficit, there are still some transformation deficits.

Level of socioeconomic development

India is still considered a low-income country, although it is progressing quite rapidly, according to commonly used development indicators. However, its level of development, measured by the HDI, does not guarantee the basic needs or freedom of choice of every citizen. India is still the country with the highest number of people living in absolute poverty (about 26% of the population). Since the mid-1970s, the incidence of poverty has declined (lately at a decreasing rate), but has recently become increasingly geographically concentrated. The progress in development was uneven; in the 1990s, the gap in social indicators between union territories grew. Poverty and social exclusion are concentrated in certain sectors (agriculture, informal sector), social groups (lower castes, tribal groups, Muslims) and territories of unions with poor economic dynamism and poor governance. Despite moderate inequality and numerous poverty eradication schemes and assertive action on behalf of the disadvantaged, there is no equal opportunity.

Organization of the market and competition

In most parts of the economy, market competition is guaranteed. With the exception of agriculture, labor and land markets, the previously high density of regulation has decreased; implementation procedures are still cumbersome. The small business sector still reserves several hundred products for exclusive production. Foreign and large local companies' regulation has been abandoned. The investment regime is now one of Asia's freeest. Indices of concentration in the sector are still high, despite efforts by the government in recent decades to the contrary. Legal procedures for the restructuring and liquidation of diseased or public companies are inadequate, time-consuming and ineffective. Shareholders ' weak protection encourages risky corporate strategies. Despite massive tariff reductions and the almost complete abolition of non-tariff barriers, trade barriers are still significant, the average tariff rate is around 26 percent (2004) and is supported by the frequent use of anti-dumping measures. Customs clearance takes more time than in competing economies. In the 1990s, privatization proceeded rather slowly, but accelerated after 1998, albeit with the almost total exclusion of state-owned enterprises.

The Indian financial system is well developed and has a high level of coverage. After 1991, it has been thoroughly reformed. State banks are still dominant, but the public sector absorbs a significant share of bank resources (41 percent) and around 40 percent of bank credit is still targeted at priority sectors. Equity capital of banks is almost sufficient to cover potential losses of non-performing loans (whose share has fallen).

Currency and price stability

For political reasons, a consequent price stability policy was followed in India (inflation tolerance was traditionally low). During the period under review, this did not change much, although high public deficits and rising oil prices made it difficult to contain inflation. India's Central Bank has always pursued a cautious monetary and monetary policy, supported by strong internal savings mobilization (by private households) and increased foreign capital inflows and remittances. Currency reserves have reached a high level of comfort. Due to its long-term nature, the level of external debt is high, but not dangerous.

Private property

Property rights are adequately defined, although restrictions on public interest are permitted in the constitution. Private property, the prerogative of private initiative and necessary to attract foreign investment, is unquestioned by governmental authorities and important political parties. The labor market is still highly regulated, there are virtually no mass redundancies or closures. That also applies to agriculture. Only in market niches is free transport, storage or pricing possible. However, some recent progress has been made in the privatization of public companies.

Welfare regime

In India, only the privileged workers of the state and formal sectors have a rudimentary social security system, although the government is now planning a guarantee of employment for the poor. These guarantees are supported by a range of central and state programs, subsidized food products, employment in times of crisis, self-help programs and integrated rural development projects. Despite efforts to improve, these schemes are still badly targeted at spreading significantly to the non-poor. Public expenditure on basic social services is, by international comparison, inadequate and does not guarantee universal coverage, without taking into account the issue of their poor quality. India is therefore not a leader in the improvement of social indicators, which show a wide difference between union territories and social groups. As a result, equal opportunities are not guaranteed: Social indicators are positively correlated with income, caste position and urban environment. Women are systematically disadvantaged, particularly in the "Hindi belt," which is shown by the extremely low number of women in the population. Low castes, tribal groups and Muslims are discriminated against in terms of land ownership and access to public sector positions, despite reservations.

Economic performance

Since the mid-1980s, the Indian economy has grown rapidly; market-oriented reforms increased this rate after 1991, despite several gaps. Due to reform resistance, there was a slight deceleration in the late 1990s, but there was a remarkable pick-up late. India is now one of the world's fastest-growing economies and could grow even more if some overly regulated markets are liberalized and subsidies and public deficits are successfully contained. This would also increase growth in labor intensity and support the dynamism of exports.

Sustainability

Extremely low health and education expenditure affects Indian development's social sustainability. This also applies to research and development, operation and maintenance and physical infrastructure upgrade expenditure. Social spending is also biased towards the tertiary sector (elite institutions and universities, urban hospitals).

Environmental quality leaves a great deal to be desired and deteriorates. The economic costs of environmental degradation are significant; according to World Bank estimates, costs range from 6% to 8% of GDP. This is mainly due to insecure water, air pollution and degradation of the soil. The poor are the most victims of this degradation of the environment. There is no lack of specific legislation or ecological movements to safeguard the environment. More activism has recently been recognized in this regard. The equation lacks adequate funding for environmental programmes, inspection and monitoring of progress (or infringements of legal provisions) and infringement sanctions. However, the total area of natural parks has increased and a new forestry policy has been implemented. In addition, companies have reduced emission levels and the courts have become more proactive in prosecuting polluters. An effort has also been made to replace diesel engines in automobiles with natural gas engines.

Management

Level of difficulty

There are no serious difficulties in India in terms of democratic consolidation. This is due to the long tradition of popular participation, the deep roots of democratic institutions, the lack of veto power of other political actors and the balancing influence of social, regional and religious conflict lines in multipositional positions. On the other hand, the government-leading majority parties faced the difficult task of consolidating a coalition of minor parties and promoting the divergent interests of relatively small constituencies without much regard for the common good. The Hindu national BJP had to balance the often aggressively formulated objectives of its front organizations (Rashtriya Swayamsevak Sangh or RSS, Vishva Hindu Parishad or VHP) to reduce the size of minority communities (by demanding a universal civil code, dismantling Kashmir's autonomy, replacing mosques with Hindu temples, etc.) and the interests of its alliance partners in order to safeguard the interests of their alliance partners. In return, the new government led by Congress was under pressure from its left-wing partners to revise the Prime Minister and his team's market-friendly economic policy, to slow down privatization and increase spending on social programs without dismantling subsidies or aggressively reducing the public deficit. State governments that make far-reaching efforts to improve governance often voted out of office. The problems at the implementation level were significant compared to moderate difficulties at a general level.

Steering capability

Faced with these difficulties, the BJP-led government and its successor demonstrated a remarkable ability to steer the country through difficult waters. The BJP had to appease its radical followers by verbally supporting their claims (e.g. in religious identity issues) and postponing any final and necessarily polarizing solution. However, this evidence of steering ability has sometimes occurred by default, namely through pressure from coalition partners on the BJP to follow a more neutral course in identity politics issues. This was also linked to the volatile path of state-level election results.

The economic policies of the National Democratic Alliance were simpler. Privatization was more aggressively pursued (against opposition in the coalition), measures were adopted to curb the massive public deficit (although it did not impose tough sanctions against government deficits) and major infrastructural schemes (road construction) were launched. However, the government could not introduce a universally valued added tax in its own ranks against the opposition.

The successive government led by Congress was less compelled to follow a secular, balanced political course and took the opportunity. The new government's economic policies were more ambivalent and included the continuation of market-oriented reforms by giving them a human face (priority for agriculture, social services, program to guarantee employment, etc.), without mobilizing adequate resources (although the Fiscal Responsibility Act was renewed), and by slowing down privatization, increasing defense expenditure and continuing to increase defense expenditure. Liberalization of foreign investments was only carried out with caution due to the resistance of leftist partners.

Resource efficiency

The government continues to inefficiently use the available financial and staff resources for the transformation project at the time of this writing. The central and state units' budget deficit is still well above 10% (not including shadow budgets, guarantees, etc.). It absorbs a large proportion of savings, eliminates private investment and reduces public investment to a level that does not guarantee the replacement of capital. The deficit is largely due to massive, in part unproductive and poorly targeted subsidies (for energy, water, fertilizer, food and oil), and increased defense expenditure and capital services. The state's tax revenue is affected by the almost complete exemption from the taxation of agriculture and the informal sector, income and corporate tax cuts and delays in the introduction of a full-fledged VAT. There is poor monitoring, alienation and poor targeting of public expenditure management. Earmarking for the operation and maintenance of facilities is far too low, contingent liabilities are not adequately addressed (for pensions and guaranteed), and budget forecasts are often too optimistic. The renewed Fiscal Responsibility Act aims to eliminate public deficits by 2008 through better tax administration, the introduction of value-added tax, the restriction of government credit guarantees and the end of central bank deficit financing.

Consensus-building

No major political party or group is questioning democratic procedures and principles. However, this does not mean that details of political tolerance towards minorities or the state's cultural identity or the pace of economic reforms are universally agreed in India. The BJP-led government tried to steer a moderate Hindu nationalist course in cultural matters by rhetorically supporting the position of its more radical followers. At the same time, they tried their alliance partners by excluding offensive items from the government program and leaving the court, civil mediators or legislature (where the opposition's consent was necessary) to resolve difficult issues. The blame could be laid on others for a lack of performance. The National Democratic Alliance had fewer problems forming a consensus on a more constructive dialog with Pakistan, since it did not question its nationalist credentials. It has indeed skillfully taken advantage of this opportunity. The efforts of the new Congress-led government to build a consensus were successful in the treatment of secessionist movements in northeastern India and Kashmir (supported by massive financial assistance for the regions concerned) and in the careful continuation of the market-friendly course by simultaneously giving in to the leftist partners on minor issues, namely the precise level of foreign participation in

International cooperation

In initiating, implementing and financing market reforms or pursuing democratic progress, international development cooperation has only a very limited part. In the future, the Indian government intends to do without foreign aid (also concerning the handling of natural disasters) and cultivates a self-confident position in contact with donors. This does not mean that union or government governments are not cooperative. Many union territories have launched far-reaching reforms in the education, health and infrastructure sector or in the overall approach to market-friendly reforms supported by international organizations. However, in principle, there is no chance of unilaterally dictated political dialogue. Liberalization and regulation of foreign direct investment is also done more with regard to local constituencies (and hesitantly) than with regard to foreign partners, although governments of all political shades recognize the need to attract more foreign investment. After the disastrous experience of the early 1990s, the government is also pursuing a cautious foreign debt policy, which is building massive international reserves as a cushion against financial risks. The government tried to become a reliable partner in the fight against international terrorism, naturally pursuing its own interests in condemning terrorist groups sponsored by Pakistan.

Democratic development

In the period from 2003 to 2004, India's relatively good ranking in terms of state monopoly on the use of force, administration efficiency, independence of its judiciary and high regard for democratic procedures did not decrease. This was partly due to default, as the coalition's main party, which ruled until the early summer of 2004, could not carry out a less secular agenda against the resistance of its smaller minority partners. Controversial projects such as the development of a universal civil code (harmful Muslims), the rewriting of historical textbooks and the "hindouisation" of education, the ban on the slaughter and conversion of cows, the revision of the constitution, etc., had to be stopped. The government was often slow or unwilling to fight Hindu chauvinism, but generally maintained a balanced position and focused its energy on maintaining adequate governance and ongoing economic reforms.

The BJP-led government, misinterpreting popular mood, called for early elections. The victory of the new alliance led by Congress in 2004 was completely unexpected; it was a kind of vengeance brought about by the progress of sections of the population (poor and farmers) and people who were uncomfortable with the policies of community agitation. It was above all the result of the Congress Party's effective building of alliances and the success of this alliance in some union territories, while some of its adherents left the old coalition behind.

The new prime minister became India's economic reforms architect Manmohan Singh. A liberal team supported him, but he was curbed in activism by market-skeptical coalition partners and the Communists ' external support. The new coalition's Common Minimum Program sought to achieve social harmony, a return to genuine secularism and labor-intensive growth. The BJP made some efforts to stop the political process by blocking parliamentary proceedings after the defeat. More troublesome in the case of attempts by the leftist coalition partners to undermine progress in economic reforms (privatization, liberalization of foreign investments, involvement of foreign experts, reform of the Provident Fund) by veiled threats to break with the government, which became more secure after the first batch of election victories in union territories.

Market economy development

From an economic point of view, the period from 2003 to 2004 was almost unmitigated. Growth in all sectors in East Asia (supported by good moons) and bullish export growth (particularly in services) increased. Growing remittances and foreign investment further strengthened the balance of payments position, which resulted in a massive accumulation of foreign exchange reserves (sufficient for one and a half years of imports). The Reserve Bank had to sterilize these to subdue inflationary pressures (which remained moderate) and currency appreciation. The traditional weak spots of economic development have remained: Massive budgetary deficits, unreliable and inadequate power supply, congestion of roads and ports, and, above all, the accentuation of disparities between the leading and lagging states, as well as almost unemployment.

Strategic perspective

The Indian government's objective is to convert the country into a developed economy by 2020 and a major player on the global scene. The chances of achieving these objectives are not bad. India has experienced rapid growth over the last decade, supported by far-reaching reforms, and the external position has improved dramatically. The rapid increase in exports of information technology services and high remittances has led to significant surpluses in the current account. This has led to a significant increase in external reserves, together with an increase in (albeit modest) capital inflows. Low short-term external debt levels provide the country with a cushion against speculative attacks.

India has made progress in reducing income poverty and many other social indicators in parallel with faster growth. The performance was uneven, however: Average income remains low and some critical social indicators have shown little movement. There is also a significant disparity in opportunities, especially for vulnerable groups in education, health and economic prospects. There has been a growing gulf between rich and poor countries in the country, leading to an increasing geographical concentration of poverty.

A strategic shift is needed to ensure a more even sharing of the fruits of growth. The new Indian government's people-friendly program is therefore heading in the right direction; this should be complemented by fiscal restraint, efforts to expand the tax network and rebalancing expenditure (by reducing unproductive subsidies) to make room for infrastructure rehabilitation, basic services, agricultural support and maintenance. It will also require dramatic improvements in basic infrastructure and investment climate to sustain past growth. Major changes must be made to ensure that basic services are delivered effectively to all citizens. In the context of decreasing water availability and increasing pollution, a long-term strategic challenge is to ensure environmental sustainability.

The country's democratic credentials are not in doubt, but could be improved by stricter federal compliance and efforts to clear the massive backlog of court litigation. The judiciary and the election committee took a pro-active course in prosecuting abusses. This should be encouraged because it will generally reduce corruption and improve the transparency of government procedures (supported by information freedom acts). The international community should encourage policies of reasonable accommodation for truly local rebel groups (in the Northeast), and efforts by foreign terrorist groups in Kashmir to destabilize peace efforts should be unambiguously condemned, as well as the prosecution of minorities (Christians, Muslims and other groups) by Hindu radicals.

CHAPTER THREE

The State and Economic Development in India

Social actors have penetrated the Indian state more than many states in East and Southeast Asia. India could neither abolish private enterprise nor embrace globalization with the same speed and ferocity, unlike China. Both complete nationalization driven by the state and globalization driven by the state would require a state that would have far greater control over interest groups such as industrialists, farmers and trade unions. Policies promoting economic growth and development in India must gradually evolve after a social consensus has been established on these policies. This is a development model driven by a relationship between the state and society, in which the power of the state was moderated by the power of social actors, even in its dominant moments.

Ideas for development were discussed in the state. Significant changes in economic policy would require building on a historic path of gradual changes in economic crises in ideas and policies. This book shows how critical this dynamic is to explain the green revolution policy and the consequent self-sufficiency of food grains and to understand the globalization of India after 1991. It is a story of gradually and circuitously increasing economic growth rates following the establishment of a policy consensus among various stakeholders. Economic crises have helped to reach a new consensus.

The growth rates of India began to look more like those of China after 2003. Figure 1 gives us a visual sense of India's growth trajectory. India's GDP grew between 1956 and 1974, when it was a closed and highly regulated economy, between 3 and 4 percent per year. The same rose to more than 5 percent between 1975 and 1990, when India's domestic private sector was given more room for manoeuvre. This was not a time when India's commitment to the global economy increased significantly (Figure 2). The shift in the paradigm in the private sector and trade orientation after 1991 was linked to higher growth rates, more than 6 percent between 1991 and 2004 and more than 8.5 percent between 2003 and 2007. It is the latter figure that drew the world's attention when, after China, India became one of the world's fastest growing economies.

FIGURE 1 India's GDP Growth

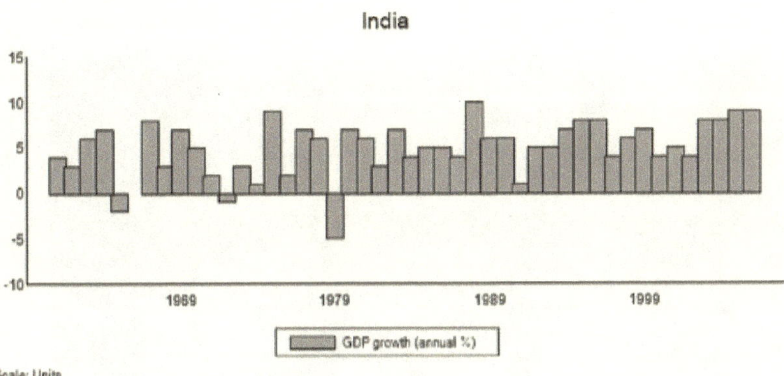

Scale: Units

FIGURE 2 Measuring India's Globalization—Merchandise Trade/GDP (%)

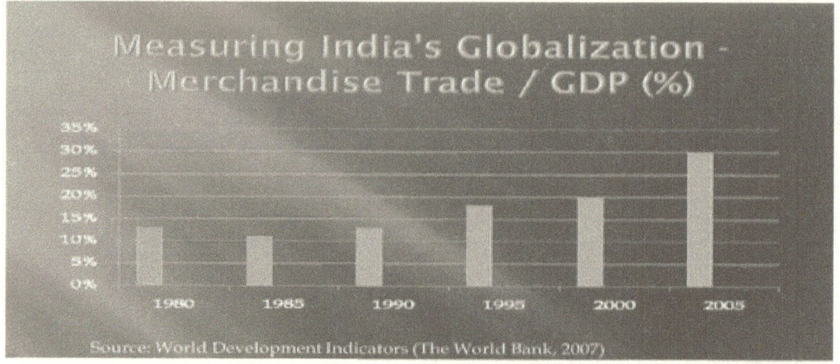

The democratic complexity of India is well known and the chaotic nature of development policy. The development state literature driven by the experience of East Asia was largely concerned with the importance of autonomy -or the ability of the East Asian state to maintain its independence from powerful social actors. India, on the other hand, has been caricatured as a country whose industrialization and growth have been hampered by politics and support. The sustained growth of India after 1991 is a puzzle for this literature.

This book will discuss the twists and turns in India's economic development policy since 1947, which gradually led to high growth. It will discuss why sectors such as telecommunications and stock markets have become efficient, while others such as the electricity sector have lagged behind. What are the socio-economic and political reasons for India's low literacy levels, the decline in Indian agriculture, the persistence of poverty and the increase in inequality in India?

The Political Economy of Growth

The state regulated India's business houses to a greater or lesser extent depending on the extent of influence they could exert within the state. The period between 1947 and 1968 was years of moderate state regulation. In comparison, strict regulation of private and foreign companies characterized the years between 1969 and 1974. In the context of low levels of growth and productivity, the state's inability to meet the demands of an increasingly mobilized population led to a gradual process of liberalization of the economy in favor of the private sector between 1975 and 1990. The significant bias in favor of government ownership and economic self-confidence that remained required the 1991 balance of payments crisis to stimulate further economic liberalization. In 1991, a technocracy convinced of the importance of globalization and private initiative took advantage of India's dependence on the IMF to focus policy attention on the Indian economy's competitiveness. During this period, India's private sector was released from significant state control. The subsequent boom in the Indian private sector was linked to high economic growth in India.

The Period of Slow Growth: 1947–74

At the time of independence, the Indian business class exerted considerable influence and played an important role in the struggle for freedom. Nationalist businesses in pre-colonial India often took positions that supported the Congress, even if this meant giving up profits in the short term. In his address at the Fourth Annual Meeting of the Federation of Indian Chambers of Commerce and Industry in 1931, Mohandas Gandhi, the man who mobilized the Indian nation to resist British colonialism, praised the role of nationalist business in the Indian freedom movement. The rich were encouraged to treat themselves as trustees of the wealth of society as a whole. Mohandas Gandhi was murdered in G's house. In January 1948, D. Birla, one of India's pioneering industries.

The powerful Deputy Prime Minister in Nehru's cabinet, Sardar Vallabhbhai Patel, was very close to G. Birla, D. At the time of independence, G. D. Birla was one of India's two leading industrialists and one who played an important role in linking Indian business to the Indian national movement. G. D. The relationship between Birla and various prime ministers is a convenient way to assess the relationship between India's state and business class.

The Sardar Sardar means Hindi's leader and Vallabhbhai Patel was affectionately called Sardar Patel was the fundraiser and organizer of the Congress Party, which was credited with bringing more than 500 princely states under one sovereign. In the early years after independence, such was his political prowess that his candidate Purushottamdas Tandon was able to defeat Nehru's candidate for Congress Party presidency. Birla funded and supported Tandon's campaign. The Sardar often stayed in New Delhi's Birla House and used Birla's goodwill in matters ranging from industrial policy to negotiations with multilateral financial organizations.

In the early years after independence, India's state and business class reached a compromise. The Indian business class wanted limited state regulation and international trade protection. Although there was agreement between the state and the business class on trade protection, there were differences of opinion on the extent of the state's economic regulation. The power of Indian business and its close relations with the state produced a regulatory regime between 1947 and 1955, which was far more attentive to the interests of Indian business than the Socialists in the Congress Party wanted. The Socialists wanted more control over private assets by the government. When they found that the Congress Party's Economic Program Committee's report (January 1948) was substantially diluted in favor of private business, they left the Congress Party in March 1948 to form the Socialist Party. The April 1948 Industrial Policy Resolution reserved exclusively public ownership in only three sectors of the Indian economy.

Secondly, there were disputes as to whether the Planning Commission was a recommendation or an implementation agency. The ministries were able to maintain their implementing powers and the Planning Commission was relegated to a largely consultative body. India's private sector was relieved to keep its distance from planning in the Soviet style. Last but not least, the Industrial Development and Control Bill, which was initiated in 1949, was opposed and reformulated into the Industrial Development and Regulation Act (1951), which gave the Indian industry a significant voice. This was the birth of industrial controls and licenses to be abolished only in 1991. The compromise between the state and the private sector that lasted until the death of Sardar Patel in 1950 was a turning point. Nehru's desire for greater economic control by the state could be fulfilled. Although Nehru saw a legitimate role for the private sector, the state would gain greater control over private activity. Nehru took a couple of years to win absolute command over the Congress Party until 1955. The 1956 resolution on industrial policy was less generous to private capital than the 1948 resolution. The Second Five-Year Plan (1956-61) increased the proportion of government investment in relation to private investment and pointed to the industrialization of heavy capital. The Nehru years saw the

Planning Commission's power increase, which earned it the epithet "super cabinet."

Nehru was not completely opposed to the private sector. It was not possible to nationalize banks. Foreign investment has continued to enjoy a favorable environment. G. D. Birla remained an important source of election funds and helped in the election years of 1952 and 1957 to mobilize the Indian industry to serve the Congress Party. During this period, Birla's business performed fairly well. The Birlas were not allowed to build a steel plant and the Tatas were not allowed to enter the automotive industry. The Birlas were allowed to produce cars and the Tatas were allowed to manufacture steel.

After Jawaharlal Nehru's death, Lal Bahadur Shastri became Prime Minister in 1964. Shastri started to systematically overturn the Nehruvian legacy quite unexpectedly. The importance of the Planning Commission has been reduced and the Office of the Prime Minister has become stronger. The National Development Council, which included leaders at state level, was also strengthened. G. D. Birla and the Indian Chambers of Commerce and Industry Federation have developed a close relationship with the new Prime Minister. Industrial sectors have been decontrolled, such as steel and cement. And during his premiership, the decision to devalue the Rupee was made. If the decision was consistently pursued to devalue the Rupee, the Indian economy's export orientation would have increased. Medha Kudaisya said that if Shastri had not died prematurely in January 1966, in the mid-1960s, the Indian economy could well have taken a private sector and trade-oriented route. This was the path followed by many countries in East and Southeast Asia.

The rest of this section will show that trade promotion may not have been easy for Shastri due to the views of most Indian businesses, intellectuals and political elites at the time. The unexpected rise of Mrs. Indira Gandhi to the Premiership after the sudden death of Lal Bahadur Shastri in January 1966 was partly due to struggles within the Congress Party, which could not be easily resolved. Indira Gandhi was known in those days to be unassertive and shy. It did not seem to pose a threat to senior leaders of Congress such as Kamraj and Morarji Desai. Mrs. Gandhi would have to strengthen her power in the party if she consolidated her position in the long term.

Over the nation's horizon, an economic crisis was looming. The 1964/65 and 1965/66 droughts and the 1965 war with Pakistan created a financial situation in which India became dependent on US PL 480 wheat shipments. A major setback for any Indian political party is food price inflation. In order to finance the Fourth Five-Year Plan (1969-74), the government needed significant external funding. Between the third plan (1961-66) and the fourth five-year plan, India's strained resources led the country to a two-year holiday plan (1967 and 1968).

The food situation and related financial situation forced India to request subsidized supplies of wheat and financial assistance from the United States. President Lyndon Johnson's policy of slow wheat shipment and the quid pro quo requested by donors was a far cry from India's liberal financial assistance during the Kennedy years. India liberalized its trade regime and devalued the Indian Rupee and submitted to external pressure.

The 1966 financial crisis and the aborted liberalization of the economy demonstrate the effects of external pressure in the absence of an internal consensus to promote trade and competitiveness in India. Indian business openly supported the reforms, but was opposed to devaluation in large part. Import substituting industry driven domestically required cheap imports for the production of goods for the Indian market. The industry was adversely affected by the increase in import prices resulting from the devaluation. The intellectual community's sentiment and views in the Indian Parliament were largely opposed to the Indian Rupee's devaluation. Such was the political opposition to the Indian Parliament's devaluation of the Rupee that Mrs. Gandhi did not even inform Congressional President Kamraj before Finance Minister Sachin Choudhury announced the measure in June 1966.

By 1969, trade promotion policy and participation in the private sector had been reversed. In areas such as insurance, banks, coal, wheat and significant parts of the steel industry, the government nationalized private sector assets. Large industrialists in the private sector were strictly controlled by the Monopolies and Restrictive Trade Practices Act (MRTP; 1969) in relation to the quantities and types of goods they could produce. Even G. D. Birla was unable to establish a relationship with Mrs. Gandhi and J. R. D. Tata was disappointed at the time.

At this time, the small-scale industrial sector flourished, with fewer regulatory bottlenecks, easy credit and some key business areas reserved for it. By reducing the foreign equity participation of foreign companies from 51 percent to 40 percent, the Foreign Exchange Regulatory Act (1974) reduced the power of multinational companies. This meant that in company boards, multinationals would have fewer powers. This eventually led to companies such as Shell, Coca Cola, IBM and Caltex leaving.

What were the reasons for this offensive against large companies in India and abroad? The Nehru, Shastri and early Indira Gandhi years of industrial policy between 1969 and 1974 look like a period of liberal economic policy. During this period, the state was ascending and private capital retreated to the greatest extent. Mrs. Gandhi understood that by undermining a group called the Syndicate within the Congress Party, which was more sympathetic to large Indian companies, she could consolidate her position as Prime Minister. When the Party of Congress decided to install N. As India's presidential candidate, S. Reddy proposed instead the name of trade union leader V. V. Giri. Indira Gandhi was afraid her opponents of the Congress would use Reddy to undermine her position. With the support of the Communist Party of India, Giri contested and won the election against the official candidate of the Congress Party. The majority of the votes in Congress went to Reddy, not Giri. Subsequently, Mrs. Gandhi's allies reigned supreme until about 1974 in the Congress Forum for Socialist Action and the Communist Party of India.

Indira Gandhi faced a political situation that after 1974 went beyond her control. The growth rate has not increased, and social unrest has occurred against both the personalization of politics and economic hardships. Mrs. Gandhi took the Congress Party in her hands and systematically undermined internal party democracy - something that was a legacy of her father Jawaharlal Nehru's struggle for independence. The controversial appointment of a Chief Justice, the ruling of the High Court of Allahabad on electoral malpractice in its constituency, low economic growth rates and a wage freeze at a time when inflation could not be controlled, all mobilized the nation against it and the Congress Party. The last straw was the proclamation in June 1975 of a national emergency or authoritarian rule. These events galvanized all non-communist political opposition forces into political solidarity -the Congress Party lost its first Janata Party election in 1977. The veteran socialist leader of the Congress, Jayaprakash Narayan, who was Nehru's close associate, gave the political movement charismatic leadership against the regime of Indira Gandhi.

The Moderate Growth Phase: 1975–90

India's accelerated economic growth, at a rate of more than 5 percent between 1975 and 1990, must be understood in the context of a steady orientation of the private sector that began in the mid-1970s and accelerated in the 1980s. In the mid-1970s, thoughts arose about the private sector and trade orientation. A special Cabinet Committee was set up in 1975 to promote exports.

A number of influential reports within India's government began to argue against the physical and financial control system and the need to promote exports. Vadilal Dagli (Chairman), Report of the Committee on Control and Subsidies (New Delhi: Ministry of Finance, 1979); Abid Hussain (Chairman), Report of the Committee on Trade Policy (New Delhi: Ministry of Commerce, 1984); Sukhamoy Chakravarty (Chairman), Report of the Committee on Monetary System Review (New Delhi, Reserve Bank of India, 1985); Narasimhan (Chairman),

Report of the Committee to Examine the Principles of a Physical Shift to Financial Controls (New Delhi: Finance Ministry, 1985).

Even in the mid-1970s, the Electronics Department established within the Prime Minister's Office foresaw the potential for India's software exports. Mrs. Gandhi was attentive in the early 1980s to China's trade-oriented growth and the Soviet system's inability to meet even its food needs. The difference between India and China was that it was politically harder for Mrs. Gandhi (1980-84) and her successor and son Rajiv (1984-89) to destroy the economic legacy built at the end of the 1960s than for Deng to destroy Mao's legacy. Liberalization in the private sector led to the gradual dismantling of private enterprise controls. The private sector of companies was highly protective. Trade orientation and significant tariff liberalization could not be achieved, and India's trade-to-GDP ratio between 1980 and 1990 remained constant.

Economic deregulation was strongly opposed. The Congress Party was largely against the orientation of the private sector. The Indian industry was so used to licensed production in the protected domestic market that the automotive industry even opposed the automatic expansion of its production capacity when it became aware that it would have to compete with a joint venture between the Indian government and Suzuki Corporation. The Monopolies and Restrictive Trade Practices Act of

1969 imposed various restrictions on large Indian companies, including the need to expand capacity. These restrictions were generally opposed by businesses and d for greater flexibility. However, the Indian industry wanted to hide behind production quotas when faced with the prospect of competition from a multinational company such as Suzuki Motors.

The Maruti Suzuki car would quickly overtake the sales of known Indian brands -the Ambassador and the Fiat cars, which for decades had not upgraded their technology. Indian industries typically became masters of "briefcase politics"-which meant bribing the government to secure licenses for production, import and export. In relation to the legacy of the 1970s, the achievements of the 1980s were quite significant. First, some industrial deregulation has been achieved in favor of the Indian private sector. Restrictions have been eased for large companies via the MRTP route. It was now easier to expand capacity or produce a product similar to a licensed product without government permission

Secondly, Rajiv Gandhi was able to move the telecommunications sector towards the orientation of the private sector. He could corporate. Corporation was a process through which the government created its own companies, which were to be run as a private company, free from political interference. Telecommunications Department (DOT) divisions in the government-owned corporate entity-Mahanagar Telephone Nigam Limited (MTNL), despite strong opposition from DOT managers and employees. The government-funded Center for Telematics Development (CDOT) began producing telephone switches superior to those produced by a joint venture between the Indian Telephone Industry in government ownership and the French Alcatel company. Despite opposition from the Indian Telephone Industries, CDOT switches had to contend with government policy to succeed. This technology has been licensed for private production and continues to serve rural areas in India. In the mid- to late 1980s, these efforts produced impressive levels of industrial growth that were only exceeded after 2003.

Third, Rajiv Gandhi made a significant effort to bring the Indian Engineering Industry Association (AIEI) closer to the government. As a result, the influential industrialists of the Federation of Indian Chambers of Commerce and Industry (FICCI), who were used to obtaining licenses by providing funds to the ruling party-a practice perfected in the 1970s, have been relegated to the background. Rajiv Gandhi consulted the AIEI on important issues, gave it access to government policy and persuaded a small association to become an organization representing the interests of the Indian industry.

Fourth, the software sector emerged as an export-oriented sector during the period of domestic deregulation. This was supported by synergies between the Department of Electronics (DOE) and India's natural comparative advantage, which was based on its technically competent, cheap English-speaking workforce. The DOE, which was housed by technocrats with similar backgrounds to the newly qualified middle-class entrepreneurs, slowly pushed the government to give entrepreneurs greater choice in terms of imports and provided easy financing for imports required for exports. It also pushed government investment in software technology parks, which provided Indian companies with cheap connectivity, office space and infrastructure, and contributed significantly to India's exports of software.

Last but not least, the Rajiv Gandhi government's most important legacy was the economic liberalization research carried out by people such as Montek Ahluwalia, Shankar Acharya, Rakesh Mohan and Vijay Kelkar in the Prime Minister's Office, the Ministry of Commerce and Industry and the Ministry of Finance. This effort was partly driven by India's own policy failures and partly by increased growth rates in China and Southeast Asia. To give an example, the successor of Rajiv Gandhi, V. P. Singh, asked his special secretary, Montek Singh Ahluwalia, to write a memo on what India had to do to grow like Malaysia. Singh and Ahluwalia have just returned from a trip to Malaysia and Prime Minister Singh has been deeply moved by Malaysia's progress. Ahluwalia's 1990 memo, leaked to the press, was a blueprint of reforms carried out by India after 1991, faced with its most severe balance of payments crisis. This view is based on interviews in December-January 2005-2006 in New Delhi and Mumbai with Montek Ahluwalia, Shankar Acharya, Rakesh Mohan and Vijay Kelkar. This research is documented in government documents such as the Union budgets and the Industrial Costs and Prices Bureau reports.

The High Growth Trajectory: 1991–Present

It is important to note that the 1991 trade, investment and infrastructure reforms were largely dependent on the path, although they were a break from the past. Without the experience of the 1970s and 1980s, there would not have been a technocratic conviction needed to break the political deadlock in favor of the biased status quo at a time of financial crisis. In 1991, India could have done what it did in 1966, retreating to reforms at a time of crisis only to pursue state control and self-sufficiency in the long term. The reason why 1991 was different from 1966 was that at the time of the balance of payments crisis, technocratic conviction in the executive branch became a virtue of reliance on the IMF and pursued tough reforms in India's political economy.

Finance Minister Manmohan Singh was a distinguished economist whose doctoral thesis was published in the early 1960s by Clarendon Press at Oxford University. At a time when most distinguished development economists spoke of the virtues of import substitution, Singh pointed out in a detailed empirical analysis that trade would be an important factor in the development of a less developed country such as India. Manmohan Singh was supported by an excellent technocratic team whose research and policy experience generated a sophisticated reform plan in the 1980s. In his 1991 budget speech, Singh stated in no uncertain terms that the underlying problem was the unsustainability of government spending in the presence of low productivity levels. The budget deficit contributed to the deficit in the balance of payments and led to pessimism among investors. The fact that Prime Minister Rao was willing to stick out his political neck in favor of economic reforms was equally important. He trusted his finance minister and understood that India's internal and external economic policies needed a fundamental restructuring at the end of the Cold War.

Why did the Indian industry agree to tariff reductions, devaluation and easier access to foreign direct investment when they opposed them in the past? Import substituting industry required foreign exchange for imports of intermediate goods, and this financing could only be provided by the IMF at a time when commercial banks and non-resident Indians withdrew their money from India. India only had two weeks of foreign exchange and no alternative financing sources when it went to the IMF in

1991. The acceptance of economic reforms by the Indian industry was articulated and effectively promoted by the Confederation of Indian Industry. Rajiv Gandhi played an important role earlier in galvanizing the AIEI into the Indian Industry Confederation (CII).

In the first three years of reform (1991-93), when India accepted conditional funds from the IMF, the technocrats, who were largely in agreement with the IMF on the three above-mentioned issues, made a necessity and pushed for far-reaching reforms in trade, industrial and foreign investment policies. The technocrats also asked for differences with the IMF. After the first year, the fiscal deficit was allowed to grow, as government spending in a poor country could not be drastically reduced. It was not possible to reform trade union laws. And market restructuring in areas such as telecommunications, stock markets and airlines has not been supported by World Bank funds from home-grown efforts. At the 1995 Gabriel Silver lecture at Columbia University, Dr. Manmohan Singh declared that India's attempt at globalization was irreversible-no matter which government came to power after the 1996 elections. This prophecy is fulfilled.

What are India's growth drivers? Industrial de-licensing after 1991 allowed private Indian companies to produce anything they liked in almost all areas without the need for a licence. For example, the Tatas, who were unable to manufacture Indian cars during the control regime, took the initiative and produced one of India's most popular cars -the Indica. They have purchased brands like Rover and Jaguar to consolidate their international business, driven by their success. The Tatas introduced the cheapest car in the world-the Nano.

Second, the Indian Rupee's devaluation made India's software and other exports more competitive automatically. To give just one example, after 60 years, India replaced Japan as the largest trader in Sri Lanka in 1996. Geography, exchange rates and better products have made Indian goods such as watches, motorcycles, cars and trucks more competitive than their Japanese counterparts. Titan watches replaced their Japanese counterparts and the cheaper Indian Kawasaki Bajaj and Hero Honda motorcycles replaced Japanese Kawasaki and Honda motorcycles.

Third, India's growing competitiveness has also arisen as a result of foreign market competition. Although India's tariffs are high according to the standards of the Association of Southeast Asian Nations, the weighted average nominal rate fell from 81.4% in 1991 / 92 to 32.9% in 1995 / 96 to 18% in 2004 / 05. India abolished consumer goods quotas in 2001. Third, the liberalization of tariffs, which was particularly successful in the intermediate goods sector, reduced the price of finished Indian products. The government and Indian companies also pushed preferential trade agreements with Singapore, Sri Lanka and Thailand to increase their competitiveness.

Fourth, it was only possible to overturn the legacy of the Foreign Exchange Regulatory Act (1974) after 1991. After 1991, non-debt investments by multinationals were seen favorably. Although foreign investment increased quite rapidly compared to the past, compared to China, this was still insignificant. A fundamental difference between the Indian and Chinese political economies is that, while China could promote foreign investment in the absence of a domestic private sector, foreign investment in India had to fight domestic companies to gain regulatory benefits. It wasn't easy. Of the 48 billion dollars that India received between 1992 and 2002, 24 billion dollars came via the portfolio route and 24 billion dollars via the direct route. In one year, the whole amount could have gone to China. And foreign investment via the portfolio route that came to India via the stock markets strengthened Indian companies. The domestic industrialist who needs foreign capital to compete with the more cash-rich Indian companies is a business lobby that supports foreign investment in India. In order to compete with richer companies such as Tata and Reliance, it was the less well-documented companies such as Bharti Televentures in India's GSM cellular sector that supported the government by increasing the foreign equity limit from 51 percent to 74 percent in 2006.

Last but not least, Indian business's entrepreneurial instincts, which could benefit from deregulation, were critical to India's growth. An important difference between India and China is that, while the Chinese economy is still largely driven by government-owned companies, its domestic private sector drives the Indian economy much more. A quick look at the list of top Indian and Chinese stock markets companies reveals this pattern quite unequivocally. Business companies in the Indian private sector have offered successful business models discussed in the world's leading business schools.

Sectors like software services and outsourcing business processes have earned India recognition as the world's back office. People in the United States think that they are "Bangalored" when their jobs are outsourced to India. The manufacturing sector in India has also started to shape after 2003. The leading sectors have been pharmaceuticals, gems and jewelry and automotive parts. Although Indian manufacturing is lagging behind China due to logistical and regulatory bottlenecks, Indian companies consolidate and multinationalize their operations, overcome domestic bottlenecks and capture the international market. For example, the Tatas bought the Tetley brand for $432 million, making it the second largest producer of packaged tea after Lipton from Unilever. Tata consolidated Tata Steel's operations in order to win the title of World Steel Dynamics ' Best Steel Company in the

World. Tata subsequently acquired the Anglo Dutch Corus Steel in 2007 for $11 billion, the fourth largest deal in the industry's history. In 2004 and 2005, the acquisition of Corus was preceded by smaller acquisitions in Singapore and Thailand. In sectors such as automotive parts, IT, consumer goods and the pharmaceutical sector, there have been significant foreign acquisitions since 2004.

Infrastructure Reforms

India has done a spectacular job reforming its telecoms, airlines, stock markets and banks. To date, it has failed to reform the power sector and has had intermediate success in reforming its ports, airports and roads. Indian Railways are becoming commercially oriented in the face of airline competition and improved roads. What is interesting is that, with the exception of the power sector, all success stories in the context of chaotic democratic politics have grown home and evolved. The success stories were driven not by privatization but by promoting competition for government-owned incumbents. Crises were crucial to the acceptance of competition by the incumbents.

The telecommunications revolution in India is truly spectacular, driven by GSM cellular technology. India adds more than 8 million telephones each month and one of the world's most efficient telecommunications services. In March 2008, India crossed the mark of 300 million lines and its tele-density grew rapidly to over 26 lines per 100 people. This remarkable success was achieved by promoting competition by getting private players to compete with the incumbents of the government instead of privatizing government assets. However, India's telecommunications boom has been much more successful in urban areas than in rural areas.

The process was quite messy as the Telecommunications Department, housed in the Communications Ministry, was opposed to competition from the private sector. It was the Office of the Prime Minister and the Finance Ministry that made the DOT bend a bit. Financial crises have spurred the promotion of competition, which was supported by the establishment of India's Telecom Regulatory Authority in 1997 and its further consolidation (2000). Each time the DOT's rent-seeking behavior brought the private sector to its knees, the Prime Minister's Office quickly moved to improve the private sector's regulatory framework. The Prime Minister took over the communication portfolio during these times.

Similar dynamics have reformed India's stock markets. Following the 1991 balance of payments crisis, the government realized the need for a well-regulated stock market. The stock market was seen as an institution that could attract savings to industrialization. There was an urgent need to curb Indian brokers ' opaque and rent-seeking propensities that required computerization and settlement system reform. Bombay Stock Exchange (BSE) brokers successfully resisted both until the Finance Ministry deployed its powers to establish a new national stock exchange (NSE). Brokers underestimated the NSE's potential. The NSE's success led to BSE reforms. Reforms in the settlement system, however, had to wait until the 2001 stock market scam, as even the regulator resisted this reform. India's health and stock markets make India an attractive destination for foreign institutional investors.

Despite the best efforts of the government, India's power sector was a dismal failure. Farmers regarded the provision of electricity as a right rather than something to be paid for. Even in the non-farm sector, there was a rampant theft of electricity. For example, in December 2007, field work in Andhra Pradesh revealed that poor and middle-income farmers were in favor of subsidized quality electricity rather than poor quality free electricity provided by Dr Rajasekhar Reddy's Congress government. They said free power came at night and the distributors did not invest in the replacement of transformers for burnt transformers or the isolation of the wires. The result was the electrocution of farmers and animals at night. Why would the Chief Minister use free electricity to make such a political deal? This could be because rich farmers could hire workers at night and pay the maintenance costs that the state-owned distributors did not provide for farmers who did not pay for electricity. The poor and middle-income farmers were also of the opinion that the government's claim to reduce theft could be foolish because agricultural consumption was not measured. At the time the interviews were conducted in 2007, Andhra Pradesh was reputed to have the best-run power sector in India. The credit rating agency Credit Rating Information Services of India Limited has consistently ranked Andhra Pradesh among the top three states for electricity sector governance due to its efficient state-owned generating companies and success in reducing transmission and distribution losses.

Challenges for Development

India's robust growth required more people. Since the mid-1990s, its agricultural sector has declined. Its trade union laws increase the Indian industry's propensity to remain capital-intensive, leading to unemployment and increased employment in the unorganized sector. Manufacturing still faces major bottlenecks in regulatory matters. Last but not least, there is much to be desired for human development in areas such as primary education and health. As a result, although the number of people below the poverty line has declined, a strategy of inclusive growth would have achieved more rapidly to alleviate poverty.

India is facing its second agricultural crisis. The first in the mid-1960s was largely due to the emphasis placed on heavy capital-intensive industrialization and neglect of public investment in agriculture in the second and third five-year plans. India corrected this prejudice after the late 1960s by attaching due importance to agriculture and increasing investment in agricultural technology, inputs and prices. Western India's middle-income and rich farmers produced the green revolution and made India self-sufficient in food grains.

India is facing its second agricultural crisis. The first in the mid-1960s was largely due to the emphasis placed on heavy capital-intensive industrialization and neglect of public investment in agriculture in the second and third five-year plans. India corrected this prejudice after the late 1960s by attaching due importance to agriculture and increasing investment in agricultural technology, inputs and prices. Western India's middle-income and rich farmers produced the green revolution and made India self-sufficient in food grains.

The Industrial Disputes Act protects less than 10% of India's workforce in a way that makes it very difficult for unionized workers to be reduced. Any industrial unit with more than 100 employees must seek government permission before firing an employee. Such permission may be difficult to obtain. As a result, most unionized workers are in the public sector and private companies are trying hard to keep workers out of the unions. Industry adapts to regressive labor laws by subcontracting its commercial operations to smaller labor law-free units and increasing production capital intensity. Although some state governments have recently favored employers with the help of favorable court rulings, a stable contract between an employee and an employee that protects the employee in return for his service has yet to develop. Inclusive growth requires intensive labor production, supported by rational labor laws.

India needed to promote a democracy that is friendly to development, transparent and investment. Despite the progress made after 1991, industrial regulations in India make it harder to make manufacturing investment in India more successful than China. Indian companies can invest in any sector, but they need permission from the state and central governments on a variety of issues ranging from land, work, environment, electricity, water, taxation and many more. These regulations often become a source of rent-seeking and patronage rather than a prompt and sensible clearance of an investment proposal on the basis of its merits. India is not an easy place to start manufacturing business unless a willing state government takes an initiative to make the investment a success. Secondly, poor ports, roads and airports serve the Indian industry negatively and are crippled by power cuts. The process of clearing investment in manufacturing must be made more transparent and less complicated.

Modi-fied India

The industrialization of India is beginning to demand more and more land. The acquisition of industrial land had to be based on the local people's consent. The acquisition had to be preceded by compensation and welfare measures that turned the acquisition of land into a developmental effort for industrial purposes. It was necessary to leave fertile double-cropped land largely for cultivation. The current laws give the government substantial powers to acquire land. The government's forced acquisition of land has led to violent unrest in some parts of India. Land acquisition has been successful in areas where developers have worked with state governments and the local people for gaining consent by attempting to uplift their human condition. States such as Tamil Nadu, Andhra Pradesh, Gujarat and Maharashtra have sought to streamline some of these sub-national procedures. Investment-friendly states can create development bureaucracies that work for local people and investors more effectively.

Indian entrepreneurship's success was in its ability to overcome and grow these bottlenecks. The software sector was particularly lucky because roads, ports, airports and power were much less needed than Indian production. India's success in creating effective telecommunications, stock markets and financial infrastructure helped it.

Inter-state inequalities increased after 1991. As the role of the central government in financing state governments decreased, the states needed to attract private investment to promote their development. Chief ministers such as Andhra Pradesh's Chandra Babu Naidu became icons of reform that tried to improve governance in their states to attract investment. They also successfully advocated development banks such as the World Bank and the Asian Development Bank for funds. Therefore, well-governed states attracted more funds while the laggards were behind. Figure 3 illustrates how inequality between states has increased since 1991. Increased inequalities will make some Indian states look like Singapore while others look like sub-Saharan Africa.

FIGURE 3 Trend in Inter-State Inequality Gini Coefficient

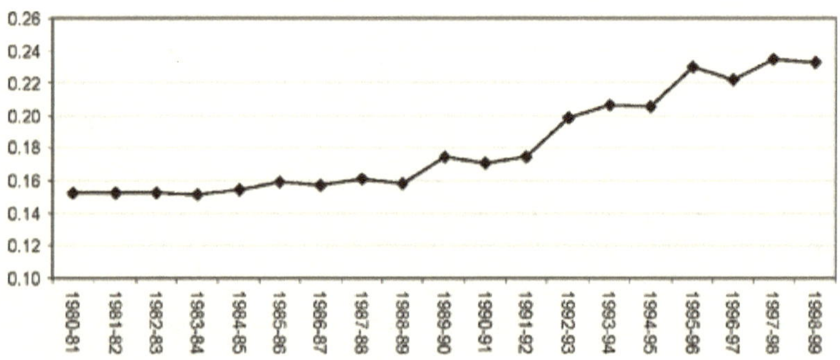

India, unlike many other Asian countries, could not ban analphabetism. Myron Weiner rightly pointed out that the Indian state's social elite tolerated child labor, which served factories and households at the expense of depriving millions of children of decent living. In areas where state and social actors worked together, literacy has improved. Success in Kerala, Goa and Mizoram was largely due to Christian missionaries' work. The recent success in Rajasthan benefited from the remarkable efforts of NGOs such as Sewa Mandir and the Center for Social Work

Research. The MV Foundation has done praiseworthy work in Andhra Pradesh to mobilize villagers and improve the condition of state-run schools.

During the reform period, India's public health record shows a dismal picture. The rate of infant mortality decreased by 30 percent in the 1980s, but in the 1990s it decreased by only 12.5 percent. Infant mortality rates in India (80/1000) were lower than in Bangladesh (91/1000) in 1990. India's infant mortality rate (71 / 1000) surpassed Bangladesh (61 / 1000) in 1999. The latest Human Development Report shows that India's poorest 20 percent infant mortality is higher than countries such as Bangladesh and Pakistan, but the same is much lower for the richest 20 percent of the population than these countries.

Deaton and Dreze point out that the number of Indians living on less than a dollar a day has fallen, although there is a substantial debate about the decline in the rate of poverty. According to a widely cited estimate, the number of Indians living on less than a dollar a day fell from 36 percent to 26 percent between 1993 / 94 and 1999 / 2000. This means that India has about 270 million people who are absolutely poor when China's figure is about 110 million.

India's growth has given the rich and the middle class more development than the poorest sections of society.

The levels of inequality measured by the Gini coefficient in India are lower than China, the United States, Singapore and Latin America, but higher than Pakistan, Bangladesh and Europe. This comparative image emerges from the UNDP's web-based map of inequality. India's growth has increased economic inequality, which in a democratic policy will be difficult to sustain. Whether India will go the way of Europe or the United States in this regard remains to be seen.

The path of economic policies that favored growth in India depended on the path. The policy consensus favored a significant role for the state in a relatively closed economy from 1947 to 1975. During this period, private companies survived, but India's trade declined. Changes in the political consensus in favor of economic deregulation began in the mid-1970s, which paved the way for shifts in tectonic policy after 1991. Path dependence ensured that new policy ideas based on the lessons of the past took some time to become part of politics and lead to policy results. This is a story of how powerful social actors who benefit from a certain set of policies are opposed to a change in the social balance. Economic change in India may be harder, but more stable than in China, because it depends more on the gradual development of a social and political consensus in favor of change. There are similarities and differences between this story of India's political economy and that presented in India's political economy by Pranab Bardhan (New York: Basil Blackwell, 1984). While both recognize the power of social groups and the prejudice to the status quo, my story illustrates the logic of change for growth and development.

In order to move policies in a substantially new direction, the Indian state needed financial crises and technocratic conviction. This was true of the green revolution and trade, infrastructure and industrial policy changes. The conviction of technocracy was important. After 1966, India pursued agricultural reforms when faced with a crisis in the balance of payments during a severe drought. India did not pursue reforms in industry and trade at the time, because the political and technological conviction was in favor of substitution for imports. The acceptance of US agricultural advice, but not industrial and trade policy, reflected the 1966 internal policy consensus. In 1991, on the other hand, economic research and the gradual implementation of growth-oriented policy changes in the 1980s, together with the rise of China and Southeast Asia and the decline of the Soviet system, convinced the political elite that by implementing substantial reforms in trade, industry and infrastructure, they could also become part of the Asian growth story.

For India's major policy shifts, financial crises were critical. They helped to overcome political opposition to policy change by the convinced technocracy and the executive. It became clear to the political elite that support for Indian agriculture and the private sector was critical in the context of difficult budgetary constraints in 1966 and 1991. The 1966 and 1991 financial crises are crucial to explaining India's green revolution in the early 1970s and its attempt at globalization in the 1990s.

Promoting the private sector after 1991 succeeded in enabling private companies to compete with public sector companies in India rather than privatizing government-owned companies. Indian entrepreneurship quickly took advantage of the advantage of the private sector. In areas such as telecommunications and airlines, which were previously reserved for the public sector, the government sector has adapted to competition from the private sector.

India's development's main challenge is inclusive growth. Growth has unequivocally reduced poverty and improved India's human condition. But the gains of the middle and richer classes were greater than the gains of the poorer sections of society. This is evident from the fact that agricultural and human development has not matched reforms in areas such as telecommunications, banks, stock markets, airlines, trade and industrial policy. India's industrialization remains capital-intensive and knowledge-intensive at a time when more than 250 million people survive on less than a dollar a day. If India grows in this way, poverty, analphabetism and malnutrition will take longer to eradicate. In addition, slow human development progress in areas such as education and health will make it harder for India to grow in the long term.

India's high growth trajectory has become reasonably stable, which is essential for development. The debate is not whether India will grow at 6% or 4% per year. The debate is whether India will grow by 10% or 8% or 6%. This is a major achievement. It has been achieved in the context of democratic politics, where changes in policy orientation have been slow, since it is difficult to create new economic winners by not harming some social groups or classes. Rich farmers, unions, manufacturers and a large section of government officials all favored the status quo that supported a protected economy and public sector. This coalition gradually begins to promote growth and competition, as the middle class learns that the game of competition is rewarding. This could be the way in which India will overcome the status quo bias in favor of low levels of growth and development described so appropriately in India's political economy, Bardhan.

India's growth and development is challenged by bringing a larger proportion of Indians into its middle class, which is well served by markets and competition. This company demands the Indian state's active role and demands support from its society.

Modi-fied India

CHPTER FOUR

Terrorism and the economy of India

Terrorism in India and the Global Jihad

Attacks on multiple targets in downtown Mumbai at the end of November 2008 are just the latest in India's long series of horrific terrorist operations. Terrorism is a complex phenomenon with many perpetrators in India. The most dangerous terrorist threat comes from groups with intimate links to the global jihadist network in the Pakistani jihadist culture centered around Usama bin Laden and al-Qaeda and its allies. While it is too early to draw firm conclusions about the responsibility for the November 2008 attacks in Mumbai, there is a good chance that the terrorists and masterminds behind their plot are linked to the global jihad.

For over a decade, India has been a target for al-Qaeda and the global jihadist movement. India has often been listed as part of the "Crusader-Zionist-Hindu" conspiracy against the Islamic world by bin Laden and his accomplice Ayman Zawahiri. The targets of the Mumbai killers - Americans, Brits, Israelis and Indians -fit into the profile of al-Qaeda and its partners. Both bin Laden and Zawahiri talked about the "Jewish-Indian alliance against Muslims in the United States."

Earlier 2007, the National Center for Counter Terrorism noted that India had the second largest number of terrorist casualties in 2007, just behind Iraq. Now it's almost sure to have the highest number of casualties in 2008. Many different groups use terror as an instrument in India, including separatist movements in the north-east, rural Maoists called Naxalites in central and eastern India, Muslim minority extremists and Hindu majority extremists. Mahatma Gandhi himself was a victim of extremist Hindu violence. These indigenous groups account for much of the country's low-intensity violence.

But the most dangerous terror threat comes from Pakistan-based Kashmiri groups with long and intimate links to al-Qaeda and bin Laden. In the late 1980s and early 1990s, a group of Kashmiri activists, assisted by the Pakistani intelligence service, the Inter Services Intelligence Directorate or ISI, founded the group, which was linked by the initial Indian assessments of the Mumbai attack, Lashkar-e Tayiba (literally an army of pure or righteous people). Usama bin Laden was the group's early supporter and provided some of the initial funding for its launch. The ISI was an enthusiastic Kashmiri insurgency supporter and wanted to use asymmetrical warfare, i.e. Terrorism undermining Kashmir's Indian control.

Let was banned in Pakistan in 2002, but there are still a number of cover names, including Jamaat ud Dawah. Its self-professed objective is to create an Islamic state throughout South and Central Asia, not just Kashmir. Its operatives have worked closely with Al Qaeda and the Taliban in Afghanistan and there are reports that volunteers have been allowed to fight in Iraq. He has raised funds in the Gulf states like al-Qaeda. There is much debate about the extent of its ongoing relationship with the ISI. The Pakistani authorities claim that there is none, but the fact is that, despite the 2002 ban, the organization was tolerated in Pakistan. He still has leadership there and trains his fighters in Pakistani Kashmir and on the border between Afghanistan and Pakistan.

Several key Al Qaeda operatives have been arrested in Pakistan since 9/11 in safe houses managed by letters. Abu Zubayda, the first major lieutenant of al-Qaeda caught after 9/11, was arrested in a safe house in Faisalabad. Gary Schroen, who served as head of the CIA station in Pakistan and led the first CIA team to Afghanistan after 9/11, noted that "since 2002, when a raid against al-Qaeda was carried out in Pakistan, members of al-Qaeda were found to be hosted by militant Pakistanis, mainly from the letter group, Kashmir insurgency supporters."

Like al Qaeda, the letter actively recruits the UK's Pakistani diaspora. Around 800,000 strong, many with Kashmiri roots, the British Pakistani community is an attractive target for many reasons, not least because members of the second and third generation have British passports and can therefore travel more easily to the West. Let was linked to numerous terrorist attacks in India, including the massacre of dozens of Sikhs in Kashmir during President Clinton's visit to India in March 2000, bombings in New Delhi in 2005 and bombings in Varanasi and Mumbai in 2006. The Mumbai subway bombings killed over two hundred on July 11, 2006.

Bin Laden was also a key figure in the creation of another Kashmiri group working in close cooperation with global jihadists, the Jaish-e Muhammad (Muhammad Army). In December 1999, Kashmiri militants hijacked an Indian commercial airliner, IA 814, from Kathmandu, Nepal, and flew it to Kandahar, Afghanistan, which was then de facto the capital of Afghanistan's Islamic Taliban. The hijackers demanded the release of several terrorists imprisoned in Indian jails, including Maulana Masoud Azhar, for a number of previous atrocities. The hijackers were allegedly assisted by the ISI station in Nepal, the Taliban received them in Kandahar as heroes, and bin Laden reportedly planned the plot. Usama hosted the victory dinner when India reluctantly surrendered to the demands of hijackers to save the 155 hostages.

Former Indian Foreign Minister Jaswant Singh, who flew to Kandahar to arrange for the release of hostages and negotiated with the Taliban, described the IA 814 operation as a "dress rehearsal" for 9/11, as it involved so many of the same characters behind 9/11. After Azhar's release, the ISI took him to Pakistan for a hero's welcome and a fundraising tour to help establish a new group, Jem.

Jem was behind an attack on the Indian parliament in December 2001, possibly with the help of letting it. This attack was designed to create a crisis between India and Pakistan by killing the Indian government and lawmakers' senior echelon. It succeeded in provoking a tense standoff that lasted more than a year, during which more than a million Indian and Pakistani soldiers were deployed in forward positions along the border. By focusing Pakistan's army on its eastern border with India, the attack also left the western border with Afghanistan open to the retreating leadership of al-Qaeda and the Taliban, including bin Laden, Zawahiri and Mullah Omar, who fled to Afghanistan from the American Operation Enduring Freedom. It was certainly not a coincidence. Like let, in Pakistan, Jaish was outlawed, but continues to operate under different cover names. There is also much debate about the extent of its existing links with the ISI.

The attacks in Mumbai showed a sophisticated level of planning that marks another milestone in the global jihad. Multiple targets in an urban environment, trained and armed killers intended to operate in small teams or alone targeting Americans, Brits, Israelis and Indians, careful targeting of targets before the attack and the use of small boats to get close to the targets are signs of the continued evolution of terrorist planners. Hotels have long been Al

Qaeda's favorite target and allies, from the multiple hotel bombings in Amman by Al Qaeda's Iraq franchise in November 2005 to the attack on the Serena Hotel in Kabul in January and the bombing of the Marriott Hotel in Islamabad in September.

Many reports of the incident say the terrorists came from Karachi's Pakistani megacity port by sea. For a long time, Karachi has been a favorite hide from the global jihad union. The 9/11 tactical mastermind Khalid Shaykh Mohammad trained most of the Saudi hijackers in a safe house in Karachi. On the day of the attack, KSM also watched the World Trade Center towers collapse from an internet café in Karachi. The attack on the Indian parliament in December 2001 was planned and orchestrated by Karachi, possibly with the involvement of KSM.

There is still a lot to learn about the attacks in Mumbai. A captured terrorist has already confessed to being a member of let, according to some Indian reports. A number of Indian experts (for example, B. Raman) and Pakistani experts (Ahmad Rashid) suggested an al-Qaeda hand in the attacks behind let. However, we should be careful not to draw conclusions from an incomplete investigation too early. In the press accounts, there is considerable confusion and contradiction about what happened. The good news is that Pakistan has offered to support the investigation that could help prevent the very crisis between India and Pakistan that the masterminds of the plots might have wanted.

India and Pakistan have improved their bilateral relations over the last few months. Pakistan's new president, Asif Ali Zardari, made several positive statements about his desire to ease tensions with India, including a pledge that Pakistan would not adhere to the doctrine of nuclear weapons for the first time, a major change in the position of Islamabad. Trade has been opened across the control line in Kashmir for the first time in sixty years, albeit in small quantities. Zardari also promised to take control of the ISI and to stop its policy of chasing terrorism in Pakistan and supporting it. His ability to do so remains in great doubt.

Al Qaeda and its allies would see this easing of tensions as a threat to their interests, like let and jem. Today, as they did in 2001, they want conflict between India and Pakistan. They thrive on the hatred produced by the conflict between Indo-Pakistan. If they were involved in the Mumbai attacks, it would partly disrupt the possibility of relieving tensions in the subcontinent and perhaps also divert Pakistan's army from the badlands on the border with Afghanistan to the border with India, as in 2001.

India has been in the bull's eye of al-Qaeda and the global jihadist union in Pakistan and Afghanistan for over a decade. The Indian people and India's democracy were not terrified into defeat despite horrifying terrorist spectacles. In particular, the people of Mumbai have risen from terrorist attacks that would shake any other city to its core time and time again. The terrorists who attacked Mumbai tried to break the city's morality at the heart of India's economic renaissance and cultural life.

Improving India's Counterterrorism Policy after Mumbai

India has emerged as one of Islamist militants' most consistent targets in the world. Although the November 2008 Mumbai attacks attracted the most global attention, they were only the latest and most dramatic in a series of bloody terrorist incidents in urban India. For example, on 11 July 2006, terrorists plant seven bombs on Mumbai's Suburban Railway, killing more than 200 people. However, the November 2008 attacks clearly focused on the inability of the Indian security apparatus to anticipate major terrorist incidents and respond appropriately. As one prominent analyst wrote, the government's responses to the Mumbai attacks were "complete failures from India's security establishment's point of view." While some Indian analysts and politicians prefer to focus on Pakistan's role as a haven for a variety of militant groups, India's domestic counter-terrorism infrastructure needs to be dramatically improved. Improvement requires significant infusions of resources, consistency in policy and political will, which are often lacking in India.

This book outlines India's current anti-terrorism policy structure and then evaluates possible reforms. Comprehensive institutional reform will be challenging in India. The country suffers from a fragmented and inefficient bureaucracy, much less resources than developed countries, even though it faces a higher level of threat, and a political elite focused mainly on electoral politics. It is probably only a matter of time before another major terrorist attack takes place. However, with the support of India's international partners, focusing on a series of significant but distinct tasks can slowly but steadily improve India's counter-terrorism capabilities.

Domestic Structure and Capabilities

The police and internal security system in India is highly fragmented and often poorly coordinated. The federal political system of the country leaves most policing responsibilities to the states, which usually have their own counter-terrorism and intelligence units. These forces are often poorly trained and equipped, especially local police. Local staff are often hired on the basis of political support and are known for high levels of corruption.

A number of central investigation, law enforcement and intelligence agencies are also available. The Home Affairs

Ministry includes the Intelligence Bureau, the Central Reserve Police Force, the Indian Police Service and the new National Investigation Agency, while the Prime Minister is responsible for the Research and Analysis Wing and the Central Investigation Bureau. The military, which is primarily aimed at foreign threats, including terrorism, also generates intelligence relevant to domestic terrorism, and a centrally controlled National Security Guard (NSG) specializes in situations of hostage and terrorist attacks.

Joint committees, task forces, subsidiary intelligence offices and a multi-agency center ostensibly coordinate the combination of state and central authorities. All these coordination mechanisms are aimed at harmonizing the intelligence collected by these agencies and generating shared perceptions of threats and related responses, but they are often slow and complicated. States and central agencies often compete over resources and bureaucratic autonomy and cooperate with each other in a highly uneven way. Many security institutions at all levels of government are understaffed, undertrained and technologically backward in addition to these organizational challenges.

All these pathologies have been evident in the failure to prevent the Mumbai attacks or to respond appropriately. In fact, there was significant intelligence that suggests that a terrorist attack on the sea was likely and that even prominent sites such as the Taj Hotel would be targeted.

However, several key bureaucratic actors-including the Coast Guard and the Maharashtra State Police Director-General-ignored this information because it was deemed inoperative. At least some kind of preparation has been attempted by others, such as the Maharashtra Anti-Terrorism Squad. The differences in readiness highlight the extent to which the security apparatus is fragmented. Even when police in Mumbai tried to take preventive action, they lacked the manpower to keep hotels safer. Once the attack occurred, the security forces did not have sufficient equipment for night vision, heavy weapons or information about the attack sites, which resulted in a long response time and a disastrous siege.

Previous attempts at reform and improvement were largely inadequate-politicians made extensive rhetorical claims, juggled staff at all levels and repeatedly promised better coordination at national level, but key capacity has not improved. Finally, Mumbai triggered the resignation of Union Home Minister Shivraj Patil, on whose watch there had been a series of previous attacks. However, the resignation of Patil and his replacement by the more competent Palaniappan Chidambaram (who under Rajiv Gandhi worked on internal security) marks only the beginning of the necessary changes. India faces a "numerous shortcomings in its internal security arrangements"

The Nature of the Threat: Domestic and Foreign

One common response to India's counter-terrorism failures was a rapid recognition of domestic weaknesses, followed by a much more vocal demand for Pakistan to "get tough." While the role of Pakistan as a sanctuary for militants (both voluntary and involuntary) is unquestionable, India's options are relatively limited. The coercive diplomacy following the attack on the Indian Parliament on 13 December 2001, called Operation Parakram, did not prevent the continued patronage of Lashkar-i-Tayyiba and other militant groups in Kashmir by Pakistan. Pakistan's "shield" nuclear weapon makes it difficult for a credible Indian diplomatic coercive.

India's current government has learned this lesson well and has instead embarked on a coordinated diplomatic offensive that has at least produced rhetorical results. It is unlikely that military threats to Pakistan will bear fruit, even if successful diplomacy has a limited impact. Pakistan simply lacks the ability and likely will to engage in domestic policies that will significantly reduce India's threat. Therefore, the primary focus of Indian security and political elites must be to improve India's internal security apparatus. India is also facing cross-border terrorism from Bangladesh in addition to Pakistan. It is believed that attacks attributed to jihadist groups like Harkat-ul-Jihad-al-Islam (huji) were launched from the country. However, the political instability of Bangladesh and its weak state capacity make it difficult for India to shape Bangladesh's anti-terrorism policy consistently.

In addition to putting pressure on Pakistan and Bangladesh, a number of major attacks were carried out under the aegis of the Indian Mujahidin (IM) with significant help from Indian Muslims. This shows clearly that the problem is not simply that Pakistan is contained. In the wake of the bombings in Jaipur, Delhi, Uttar Pradesh and elsewhere claimed by the IM, Indian police and intelligence agencies were forced to scramble, revealing a significant indigenous capacity for terrorism. If a trend of radicalization continues among small but potentially growing portions of India's Muslim community, strengthening domestic intelligence will become increasingly central. Although pockets of radicalization were uncovered as far south as Kerala, it seems that the primary recruiting grounds for Islamist radicals were urban areas in north and west India.

India is therefore facing threats from porous borders and weak governments to the east and west. These foreign threats combine to create a dangerous situation with a troubled internal security apparatus and some level of domestic radicalization.

The Path Forward: Coordination and Capacity-Building

The main domestic response to Mumbai focused on streamlined coordination between agencies across state and federal lines and the establishment of a new National Investigation Agency (NIA). The NIA aims to empower a federal agency to investigate major crimes such as terrorism and organized crime without the need for states to do so. Special courts will be able to hear cases related to terror quickly. New staff from existing intelligence and law enforcement agencies across India will complete the NIA. The infusion of funds and staff into the overall security apparatus was also promised, and the NSG was deployed across the country to provide a faster response to future attacks. These steps are a useful start. However, these efforts alone will lead to little significant results if they do not have three main characteristics.

First, they must be maintained for a long time. It is a task of at least half a decade, and probably longer, to dramatically strengthen the institutional capacity of India's counter-terrorism apparatus. Training new and current staff alone is an enormous task, much less equipping them properly. A new federal agency or set of laws will make little contribution to this fundamental task unless they can maintain the momentum needed for years of unglamorous but crucial training and institution building. Locking budgetary approval lines over a 5-10-year period will be critical in order to prevent the effort from falling victim to domestic politics and election vicissitudes.

Secondly, there must be adequate resources for reform efforts. India is a poor country with many pressing needs, and the lack of wealth in India reflects security funding. India simply does not provide sufficient money per capita for its security agencies compared to the budgets of even much smaller developed countries. This leads to undertraining and understaffing of their staff, leading to corruption and reliance on crude and often counterproductive police techniques. International assistance could reduce the impact of this reform on India's budget in the form of grants to train and equip police forces. Large-scale international aid is unlikely in the current economic environment, but small measures could make a significant difference, especially if they focus on the cities most likely to be attacked in the future (Delhi and Mumbai).

India's political leadership must finally exercise the will to push past bureaucratic and state-centric rivalries. This is an enormous challenge for a political class focused primarily on India's cutting-edge electoral competition. Despite these challenges, it is essential to maintain a degree of consistency and follow-up so that the reform process does not stop or waste enormous amounts of time and money. In bureaucratic battles over turf, resources and responsibilities, government ministers must not allow themselves to be used as pawns. The power to oversee the security apparatus must be given to specialized task forces led by elected officials and supported at the highest levels. This will involve overcoming the police and intelligence agencies' traditional aversion to transparency.

Given these profound challenges, Indian leadership is best advised to manage a couple of separate projects-firstly, on the basis of short-term coordination changes that can leverage existing assets and capabilities, and secondly, on the basis of a much longer and broader task of improving training and technical capacities across India's security apparatus. Conflate the two into one major reform agenda will likely slow down and undermine the overall effort. India must carry out a series of discrete, manageable tasks if it is to strengthen itself against the threats from both the border and its own people.

An American Role

In strengthening India's anti-terrorism capabilities, the United States can play a helpful role. The United States has already cooperated extensively. In the wake of Mumbai, the Federal Bureau of Investigation and Indian Security Services illustrates the dramatic improvement in Indo-U.S. relationships. Intelligence sharing with India has also increased, most of which are obviously linked to Afghanistan and Pakistan.

The relationship should go beyond research collaboration and sharing of intelligence into a broader training and capacity building project. One of the U.S. law enforcement agency's traditional strengths was training police and domestic intelligence forces in other countries. India would benefit enormously from even a small, but sustained program to train Indian police in the United States and send American trainers to India to speak about successful practices. This could be a small program to provide state and federal police with specialized training.

Even basic training would increase India's domestic security forces ' professionalism. In addition to helping prevent terrorist attacks and responding to them, increased professionalism could reduce the resentment of security forces in parts of the Indian Muslim community, which view the police as indiscriminate and brutal. Small but meaningful grants for training and equipping police forces could also be provided.

Preparing for the Inevitable

Even if there are major reforms and Indo-U.S. Cooperation is emerging, but India is likely to be hit again by a major terrorist attack. One of the key challenges after the event will be to avoid another cycle of institutional reform that is rhetorically compelling but under-resourced and soon forgotten. Further risks of a crisis in Indo-Pakistan will spiral out of control following a dramatic incident.

The United States and India's other partners can be a constituency that advocates a certain degree of continuity in order to avoid disruptive policy shifts that undermine imperfect but existing reform efforts while actively trying to reduce subcontinental tensions. The process of strengthening the capabilities of Indian counter-terrorism will be long and difficult and will probably not bring any sudden successes, but it is nevertheless essential.

Current happening on terrorism (India and Pakistan)

Prime Minister Narendra Modi is under heavy pressure from his supporters to punish neighboring Pakistan for a suicide attack on an Indian paramilitary convoy that killed at least 41 soldiers in Kashmir, with India's national elections barely months away. India blamed neighboring Pakistan squarely for the bombing, which India accuses of supporting Kashmir militants. Pakistan denies the accusation.

Modi took the following to deal with terrorism in India:

Diplomatic isolation

India's first public reaction to the attack was to withdraw Pakistan's most favored national trade status and take all possible diplomatic steps "to ensure complete isolation from Pakistan's international community." New Delhi insists "there is unquestionable evidence that (Pakistan) has a direct hand in this horrific terrorist incident." India's foreign ministry on briefed diplomats from key countries based in New Delhi, including China, which in the past blocked India's proposal to list Chief Masood Azhar of Jaish-e-Mohammed as a United Nations terrorist. The ministry called on Pakistan to take "immediate and verifiable action against terrorists and terrorist groups operating from its controlled territories in order to create a favorable atmosphere in the region free of terror."

Military strikes

India's army said it carried out a campaign of "surgical strikes" against militants across the highly militarized border that divides the Kashmir region between India and Pakistan after an attack on an Indian army base in 2016 that killed 19 soldiers. Pakistan rejected reports that India's military targeted "terrorist launch pads" in the Kashmir part administered by Pakistan. Islamabad instead said that India had killed two of its soldiers in "unprovoked" firing across the border.

After the latest attack -the worst in the history of Kashmir -Modi warned that those behind the attack would pay a heavy price and that the security forces were given a free hand to act against terror. The Times of India newspaper reported Saturday that the military options -short of two nuclear-armed rivals going to war -could range from "subterranean attacks and the occupation of some heights along the line of control (ceasefire line) to restricted but precise air strikes against non-state targets in Kashmir, which is run by Pakistan."

India's former high commissioner for Pakistan said it couldn't discuss a possible military response in public. "we said Pakistan is going to pay a price. For obvious reasons, we will not explain how this cost would be imposed." -Paul Staniland, a professor of political science and an expert in South Asia at the University of Chicago, said Pakistan's army assumes that it will be attacked and that Indian forces are preparing for a serious incursion of some kind.

Domestic pressure

Indian analysts say that no political party can afford to disregard public opinion before Indian elections. Protesters have already chanted "Attack Pakistan" and fiery debates on TV channels have called for retaliation. "it's a very tense situation." The country's mood is very angry at what happened. And there are also elections in the offing. No party could afford to disregard public opinion"

India's stakes were too high to not do anything. "Modi is in a very difficult position. Indian forces are quite capable, but what kinds of strikes would achieve the core goal is not clear. Kashmir and Pakistan are among the few issues of foreign policy that have a real electoral resonance."

US response

In a statement condemning the attack, the US identified Pakistan and said it strengthened US determination to strengthen cooperation on counter-terrorism with India. The US has offered to sell unarmed Guardian surveillance drones, aircraft carrier technologies and F-18 and F-16 fighter aircraft in order to improve India's military capabilities. However, there are clashes, including India's purchase of Iranian oil and the Russian S-400 ground-to-air missile system, which could trigger US sanctions against India.

The Himalayan puzzle

Since the Himalayan territory was divided between India and Pakistan shortly after the two arch-rivals gained independence in 1947, Indian-administered Kashmir has remained a challenge for Indian policymakers. The territory was at the heart of two of India's four wars against Pakistan and China. Human rights groups say that India responded with disproportionate force to public protest while treating the Kashmiri self-determination struggle as the proxy war of Islamabad against New Delhi.

Initially, New Delhi dealt with largely peaceful protests against India. However, a series of political blunders, broken promises and a crackdown on dissent led to the eruption of Kashmir in 1989 in a full-blown armed rebellion against India for a united Kashmir, either under Pakistan's rule or independently of them. The conflict has intensified since Modi came to power in 2014 amid rising attacks by Hindu hardliners against minorities in India, further deepening frustration with New Delhi's rule in Kashmir. The nationalist government led by Modi's Bharitya

Janata Party has tightened its position against both Pakistan and Kashmiri separatists.

Modi' Move on Pulwama Attack

Indian fighter jets crossed the control line before dawn on Tuesday 12 days after the Pulwama attack and carried out "non-military, pre-emptive air strikes" in Pakistan to target the Jaish-e-Mohammed terrorist group's training camp, the largest escalation in decades between the two countries. Two weeks ago, in the deadliest attack on security forces in Kashmir, the Jaish-e-Mohammed killed 40 soldiers in Pulwama.

At approximately 3.30 am, the Indian Air Force's 12 Mirage 2000 fighter jets crossed the control line and dropped 1,000 kg of bombs at a vast terror training facility in Balakot, which was the hub of training in suicide attacks, government sources said. Foreign Secretary Vijay Gokhale said several terrorists, trainers and Jaish commanders planning more terrorist strikes in India were killed. Some 300 terrorists were killed, including the brother-in-law of Jaish chief Masood Azhar, sources said. But no official figure has been released by the government.

Hours after India confirmed the air strikes, Prime Minister Narendra Modi said at a rally in Rajasthan: "I assure you, the country is in safe hands." India stressed that the strike was based on "very credible information about intelligence" that JeM (Jaish-e-Mohammed) was planning terrorist strikes in India. This made "this strike absolutely necessary. It was a pre-emptive, non-military strike," the Foreign Secretary said. Pakistan Prime Minister Imran Khan chaired an emergency meeting, after which Islamabad said in a statement: "India has committed an aggression that Pakistan will respond to at the time and place of its choice."

It was said that Maulana Yousuf Azhar, or Ustad Ghouri, Masood Azhar's brother-in-law, headed the Balakot camp in the thick forests and on a hilltop. Yousuf Azhar was one of the terrorists involved in the hijack of flight IC-814 from Indian Airlines in 1999, in which passengers from Kathmandu to Delhi were held hostage in Kandahar and swapped for Masood Azhar, who was in India's custody. For the first time since 1971, the Indian Air Force has crossed the control line. Operation Balakot marked a shift from the traditional matrix of hostilities between the two countries, said former top bureaucrats, and emphasizes India's message to Pakistan that the cost of not acting against terror on its soil will be heavy.

Following the attack of Pulwama on February 14, it was decided at a meeting of the Cabinet Security Committee chaired by PM Modi that India should send a strong message, sources said. "Credible intelligence has been received that Jaish-e-Mohammed attempted another suicide terror attack in different parts of the country, and fidayeen jihadis (suicide bombers) were trained for this purpose," the Foreign Secretary said. "India has shown many times that it is seeking action against Jaish-e-Mohammed and others in terror camps that are so large that they can train hundreds of jihadis and terrorists at any given time.

The strikes were "100 percent successful" and continued "exactly as planned", adding that the planes returned scratchlessly. Pakistan tried to scramble the F-16, but the Indian jets were unable to engage. India has briefed major world powers on the air strike, which has led to strong statements from countries such as Australia and France. China, which calls itself the "all-weather ally" of Pakistan, urged "both countries to restrain themselves." During the Kargil conflict in 1999, the last time tensions were at such a high level between the two countries. The army carried out surgical strikes on terrorist launch pads across the control line on 29 September 2016 in retaliation for an attack on its base in Jammu and Uri in Kashmir earlier that month.

Security improvement under the Modi administration

Since the Modi regime came to power at the centre, the Indian Army has shown a strong improvement that carries on the vision of much-needed army modernization to keep pace with the constantly changing art of modern warfare. This modernization is consistent with the Army's policy of "ensuring the army's capacity and operational efficiency to meet all current and emerging challenges." Infantry has continuously been overlooked since the UPA government came to power with little or no development at the level of infantry, especially under AK Antony, the former Minister of Defence. This led to the cancelation of many arms trials and tenders to replace outdated arms with an active policy of importing much-needed arms, as well as multiple scams, such as agustawestland and OFB scams, and the blacklisting of companies that led to many pending projects falling into the limbo. Under the NDA regime, the level of infantry equipment was significantly improved, with more than 50,000 bullet-resistant vests ordered from different manufacturers in a short time, and more than 1.86 Lakhs bullet-proof vests ordered from an Indian private company SMPP.

Night Vision devices have been purchased in high numbers such as BEL Night Vision Goggles, Passive Night Sights, Tonbo EK and Arjun Thermal Sights to improve the ailing condition of Indian Night Fighting Capabilities. The Israeli company FAB Defense, TDI Arms and OFB are now upgrading older weapons such as AK-derivatives with Picatinny Rails, Quad Rails, Foldable Buttstocks, Cheek Rest and Foregrip to mount various accessories such as Red Dot and Holographic Sight in an overall better ergonomic experience for the operator. The older INSAS 1b1 rifles are also upgraded with cheek rests and a Top Accessory Rail for different optics such as Night Vision and Telescopic Scopes. The Indian Army has also launched a requirement for fast purchases of nearly 2.5 chambered Lakh Battle Rifles for 7.62mm NATO and 6.5 chambered Lakh Assault Rifles for 7.62x39mm. These will replace the older INSAS with contemporary weapons in service with the Indian Forces. The Indian Army will also purchase 93,000 Carbines, including 5719.338 Lapua Magnum Sniper Rifles. The omnipresent Gypsy Utility Vehicles will soon be replaced by TATA Safari Storme, which is inducted in considerable numbers in the Indian Army. About 1500 + TATA Safari Storms were rolled out of a total of 3192 ordered by the Indian Army for the Indian Army. In addition, the Indian Army has ordered many vehicles to replace old and old vehicles such as Ashok Leyland FAT 6x6 (450 units ordered), 4x4 Ambulances (825 units ordered), TATA Multi-Axle Trucks (1200 units ordered), TATA Xenon Pickup (more than 500) and Force Gurkha 4x4 Light Strike Vehicles.

Artillery:

After overcoming the Bofors Deal ghosts, the Indian Army finally ordered its first artillery pieces, as it placed a 39-caliber towed artillery gun for some 145 M777 155 mm at a cost of $737 million. In addition, for the Indian Army, which will be manufactured in India, 100K-9 VAJRA-T Self-Propelled Howitzers have been ordered. The Defense Acquisition Council (DAC) has also cleared 150 Advanced Towed Artillery Gun Systems (ATAGS) 155 / 52 Caliber Artillery Guns with nearly 1200 ATAGS and 600 + Dhanush. The OFB also upgraded the Indian Army's 130mm Field Guns to 155mm and bagged 300 such guns in service with the Indian Army. The NDA regime was the largest shot in the arm for the Indian Artillery Arm, which in technological and numerical terms continuously lost its edge over its adversaries. The Indian Army also induces many more multi-barrel rocket launcher systems from Pinaka and hopes to induct 22 such systems by 2022. The new chassis for 9K58 Smerch Rocket Artillery Systems will also be Ashok Leyland 10x10 HMV.

Helicopters and Drones:

The DAC has cleared the purchase of 6 AH-64E Apache Helicopters for the Indian Army at a cost of Rs 4,168 crore with AGM-114R-3 Hellfire-II missiles, Stinger 92H Air-to-Air missiles, AN / APG-78 Fire Control Radars and maintenance as part of the agreement. In addition, the Indian Army has projected a requirement for 114 Light Combat Helicopters with an already issued RFP for 15 lchs. India has also entered into an agreement under the NDA regime for 133 Ka-226T helicopters to replace the older Alouette III helicopters and their derivatives in service with the Army Aviation Corps. The Indian Army is also ordering unmanned drones for surveillance purposes, such as NETRA Quadcopter Drone and DJI Phantom, developed indigenously, together with Israeli spylite mini surveillance drones for infantry units.

Special Forces:

Special Forces have also seen a major upgrade during the NDA regime since the Special Forces occupied an important position in the aggressive attitude of the NDA against the sponsorship of terrorism by Pakistan. The Special Forces of the Army have upgraded their older rifles such as Tavors and Kalashnikovs, along with the acquisition of new weapons systems such as Carl Gustav M4 Recoil-Less Rifle and Sako Tika Sniper Rifles alongside Beretta 92 guns. Modular plate carriers, surveillance drones, communication devices and state-of - the-art night vision devices are now induced to bring the gear level to level 1.

Air Defence Systems:

The medium-range surface-to-air missile system and Akash-1 / 1S surface-to-air missile systems were installed in the Indian Army to strengthen the capabilities of the Army Air Defence. In addition, the guns L/70 and Zu-23 have been upgraded and more modern Air Defense guns are now on the procurement proposal "Buy & Make Indian." Empowerment to purchase additional stockpiles of weapons in rapid procurement has given Army, a much-needed ability that it did not have in previous regimes, often leading the Army Cheifs to write letters to PMO. 21 veterans of the Lakh Army also benefited after NDA came to power, with the implementation of OROP. Punitive actions against Pakistan at the local level and success in counter-terrorism operations have added to the army's morality in the uncertain challenges of warfare in the 21st century.

Army's' Make in India ' program aims to develop indigenous weapons that are a high ambition to reduce dependence on imports. The Modi regime was a much-needed shot in the arm for the Indian Armed Forces in general and the Indian Army in particular, as the Army is now achieving the highest level of operational readiness by clearing the acquisitions of Rs.2 Lakh Crore, which speaks volumes about the increased capabilities.

CHAPTER FOUR

India and the world: Foreign policy in the age of Modi

The foreign policy of Prime Minister Narendra Modi was characterized by great energy, a desire to break the mold of the past and a desire to take risks. Foreign relations should have produced more significant results in view of the vigor it has imparted. They didn't. This is not only due to the poor design and implementation of certain initiatives, but also to the fact that external variables are outside your control in foreign policy. Some foreign policy trends had hardened even before the Modi government took office in May 2014. 1) The process of resolving India's border issue with China by the Special Representative reached a dead end. 2) The same happened with Pakistan's composite dialogue. In fact, without Pakistan's efforts to punish the perpetrators of the November 2008 Mumbai terrorist strike in Mumbai, the very basis of a bilateral dialog was undermined to resolve issues.

What has Modi sought in his foreign policy?

Through its publicly publicized Raisina Dialogues, the Modi government has put forward themes that it wants to pursue in its foreign policy. "Connectivity" was the overarching meme associated with its desire to push neighborhood ties in its first iteration in 2016. The dialog was conducted in January 2017 under the heading "Multipolarity and Multilateralism," indicating India's broader vision as a regional power. But they don't tell the whole story. In its great strategy, India can only have one major objective-to promote economic growth and secure its periphery. In this respect, it is logical to integrate the South Asian economy through enhanced connectivity, although it is pursued fittingly, mainly due to India's poor ties with Pakistan. In order to secure its periphery, New Delhi must face its greatest challenge in foreign policy -moderating, if not breaking, the alliance between China and Pakistan. In the absence of this, it remains limited to sub-optimally managing its relationships with the two. As of today, however, even in this task, the Modi government seems to be faltering.

Early momentum

Modi arrived with a great drive. He had made nine foreign visits in the seven months he was in office in 2014. He has visited 36 countries in his two-and-a-half years, a handful twice, and the United States four times. A remarkable aspect of his visits was that he was in many cases the first PM to visit a country, even key neighbors, in years-the first in 17 in Nepal, 28 in

Sri Lanka, 34 in the United Arab Emirates, and the first in Mongolia. Modi came to power with an agenda of "first neighborhood." He signalized his commitment by inviting all SAARC leaders to his inauguration as Prime Minister. His first bilateral visit to India's "best friend" Bhutan in June 2014 and his second visit to Nepal in August. In November, he returned to Kathmandu to attend the 18th SAARC summit, where he carried out an important visit to Pakistan's Prime Minister Nawaz Sharif.

The neighborhood pattern was repeated in 2015, but this time it focused on the Indian Ocean when visits to the Seychelles, Mauritius and Sri Lanka as well as Bangladesh and Afghanistan took place. All five Central Asian "stans" were a second important cluster in July 2015. With Modi's 2016 visits to Saudi Arabia, Iran and Qatar, a third set of priorities became visible. In August 2016, he had already visited the UAE, and Crown Prince Mohammed bin Zayed al Nahyan became the chief guest at the 2017 Republic Day parade. All these were underlying visits to Japan and different European countries in order to attract investors and aid. The visits to the United States were a special category aimed at strengthening ties with the only country that could help India to offset Chinese power and whose friendship opened the doors to many other countries and institutions.

The best laid plans...

Somehow in the neighborhood things didn't work out as well as they could-and we don't even talk about Pakistan. At the 18th SAARC summit in Kathmandu, it was evident that Islamabad was unwilling to support the connectivity projects being mooted and that Sharif was hobbled by the army domestically. By 2016, the situation between India and Pakistan reached a point where a boycott led by New Delhi led to the collapse of the 19th SAARC summit in Islamabad.

Nepal's ties nose-dived in 2015 following the promulgation of a new constitution that militated against Madhesi or plains people's interests. New Delhi woke up at the last minute and sent the situation back to Foreign Secretary Jaishankar, but it was too late. Eventually, a road blockade softened the Nepalese, and a constitutional coup backed by New Delhi led to a break in the alliance between the CPN (UML) and the CPN (Maoist) in Nepal and the replacement of K P Sharma Oli by Pushpa Kamal Dahal (Prachanda) as prime minister. But the damage was deep, and with some Chinese encouragement, Oli is now fanning the flames of Nepali nationalism.

The new Indian affirmation was also visible in Sri Lanka, where New Delhi helped cobble an alliance that saw Mahinda Rajpakse's defeat in the presidential election. Due to the growing links between Sri Lanka and China, the man who defeated the LTTE became anathema to New Delhi. But New Delhi was more alarmed by the 2014 and 2015 docking of Chinese submarines at Colombo harbour.

There was no visit to the Maldives as New Delhi's relationship with Male remained deadlocked following the removal of Mohammed Nasheed as President and President Abdulla Yameen's steady consolidation of control. But visits to the Mauritius and Seychelles island republics were useful in developing India's maritime domain awareness scheme, as well as its naval position in the Indian Ocean.

The elephants in the room

The big failures in the ties between India and Pakistan are related to China. India-Pakistan has never really got off the ground after a kind of thaw in 2014. There were incidents on the control line, and the new government sought to clearly signal its tough intention by carrying out an unprecedented counter-bombardment at the site.

But on Islamabad, New Delhi didn't give up. In early December 2015, after the Ufa meeting between Sharif and Modi, their nsas met in Bangkok. Later on Christmas Day, the birthday of Nawaz Sharif, Modi made a surprise descent on Lahore to wish him personally.

However, the attack on the Indian airbase at Pathankot, a week later on January 1, 2016, changed Pakistan's Indian narrative. Since then, Prime Minister Modi has repeatedly called on Pakistan to be sanctioned as a state terrorist sponsor and isolated by the international community. The September 18, 2016 Uri attack and the Indian response to the so-called surgical strikes ten days later on September 28 / 29 indicate that India and Pakistan are returning to the future. Modi's obsession with Pakistan's "terrorism" is puzzling, as we haven't suffered a massive civilian casualty attack since 2011. It seems to be intended to appeal to the domestic electorate.

Nothing so dramatic happens with China. Indeed, China's "transgressions" on the line of actual control have actually decreased to just one metric. The last such major event was the peculiar drama that played in the Chumur sector during Xi Jinping's state visit in September 2014. But the border talks have stopped and there has been no significant political or economic outcome from either the 2014 Xi visit or the 2015 return visit of Modi.

However, the CBM regime ensures that its disputed border does not trigger conflict, while India participates in initiatives led by Beijing, such as the Asia Infrastructure Investment Bank (AIIB) and the Shanghai Cooperation Organization (SCO) and the BRICS, and implements cooperation motions.

India's natural ally

In its relations with the United States, India has had unalloyed success. This is not because we have an identity of interests, but because the other can meet the needs. India needs the world's leading military power to maintain a balance against China, while the US needs India, as it is the only credible partner to build a coalition in East Asia to confront China. These ties were not an initiative of Modi, but emerged during George W Bush's presidency. In fact, it may be that the result was sub-par given the momentum.

Relations with Japan are a subset of ties with the US and once again serve mutual needs-India wants Japanese investment and technology, while Tokyo wants India to be part of the East Asian coalition. What about the main agenda: Seeking India's economic transformation? Modi's foreign visits have led to a sharp rise in FDI to India, according to the government. India, for example, attracted $44 billion in 2015, a 29% jump over the previous year's figure. The figure may be higher in 2016, but it should be remembered that the figure for 2012 was $46.55

billion, so it would be a mistake to attribute growth to Modi's foreign policy alone.

Modi also participated in multilateral forums such as the BRICS, the East Asia Summit and the G-20. The political part of the agenda, however, was often more important than the economic one. For the Modi-Sharif meeting, therefore, the Ufa BRICS summit became more important than the substantive agenda. Because of its support for terrorism, the BRICS summit in Goa in October 2026 was an opportunity to corner Pakistan.

Looking ahead

India's economy will remain a growth magnet and attract foreign investment, despite the self-inflicted demonetization wound. But the story of India can be affected by questions about its government's competence and whimsical ways. More importantly, there are concerns about its failure to carry out much-needed domestic reforms to ease India's business rules. Modi appears to be on a permanent election campaign, unable to take the hard decisions necessary for the next wave of reforms. India's concerns remain undiminished. Pakistan, far from being isolated for its support for terrorism, receives greater attention due to the compulsion of major powers such as the United States, Russia and China to achieve peace in

Afghanistan. Indeed, the agreement between Russia and Pakistan and the relationship between Russia and China pose disturbing questions for New Delhi.

In South Asia, China is still swarming over us. The latest sign was Xi Jinping's aid, loans and investment commitments of $24 billion during his 2016 visit to Bangladesh. As it is, the Bangladesh military's three wings are equipped with Chinese equipment. Indian aid to Nepal has declined, while China has now pipped India as the top donor of aid. More worrisome are the internal trends suggesting growing Chinese influence in the country. The new Srisena government promised to review many of the alleged pro-China actions, but it is clear that no real change has taken place as time passes. Chinese influence is now a growing reality to be taken into account in Sri Lanka by India.

India considered itself a player in Central Asia in the mid-1990s, but the Chinese have swamped everyone today, including the US and Russia. Compared to India's approximately $1.3 billion, Chinese bilateral trade with the region exceeds $50 billion. China's banks hold a significant share of several "stans" government debt. And Chinese pipelines and railways turn the region away from its historic links with Russia. India's foreign policy has a major problem with its illusion that it somehow competes with China. We are surely China's upcoming rival, the only one with enough physical size and population to offset its power. But we're a long way from making the potential come true. We urgently need a strategy to do this in the meantime. Because of the enormous difference between India and China in economic and military power, we need asymmetrical means of dealing with Beijing. We have significant soft-power assets, but they can only be effective with the real hard-power currency -cash and exportable military goods.

India's broad foreign policy thrust remains legitimate and valuable. But what is needed is restraint and concentration. We can't take China on board. India's neighborhood in South Asia is a priority, and Modi's access to the Persian Gulf is of great value because it is India's most important external region. It is where most of its oil is obtained and where 7 million citizens return substantial remittances. Saudi Arabia, the United Arab Emirates and Qatar have huge sovereign wealth funds that always seek good investment destinations. India must not only have access to these funds, but also establish security links to secure its oil and nationals.

The Chah Bahar project offers us a relatively inexpensive response to the One Belt One Road strategy by enabling a multi-modal link between Iran, the Caucasus and Russia with Europe. We can also be in the connectivity business if we can provide subcontinental and Indian Ocean links. Although the first indications are that there may be opportunities in the Trump era, caution is necessary because at this juncture too many imponderables are at play. However, real success for Modi's foreign policy will require an effective domestic policy that focuses mainly on investment and economic growth. This requires not only vision-which Modi has in surface-but competence and execution, which appears to be lacking.

Russia's recent agreements and defense cooperation with Pakistan shook New Delhi and led to the ties between the two countries being repaired. Both leaders, PM Narendra Modi and Vladimir Putin, chose the same "informal" format to reset ties in Sochi, a Russian city located on the Black Sea on May 21.

Wuhan breaks the deadlock

Coming from the Indian-Bhutan-China tri-junction of the Doklam standoff between India and China, the Wuhan Summit was a useful, timely and necessary step in reducing the negativity built up in their ties. Both countries sent the right signal to revive relations and create a positive atmosphere while working on their differences with the summit. Since this was an informal summit, the objective and agenda were not stated. The leaders therefore enjoyed a free-wheeling conversation, which provided a broad context for the summit and outlined future efforts for cooperation.

Indo-US 2+2 dialogue

The first edition of the 2 + 2 dialog between India and the United States took place in New Delhi after a couple of postponements. Known as the second highest level of engagement between the two countries following the engagement at the summit level between the Prime Minister and the President of the United States, this is an essential mechanism that saw Minister of Foreign Affairs Sushma Swaraj and Minister of Defense Nirmala Sitharaman hold extensive talks with US Secretary of State Michael R. Pompeo and Secretary of Defense James Mattis. Both sides signed the Indian Communications Compatibility and Security Agreement (COMCASA), which provides a legal framework for the United States to separate its sensitive communications equipment and codes, enabling India's security establishment to collect operational information in real time.

India against biological and chemical weapons

India became the Australia Group's 43rd member, which aims to prevent the proliferation of biological and chemical weapons, ensuring a safer world. India is a member of three of the four export control regimes of nuclear power. India joined in 2016 the Missile Technology Control Regime (MTCR) and in 2017 the Wassenaar Arrangement (WA). India's Nuclear Suppliers Group (NSG) membership bid is pending as China opposes India's bid.

India-Japan and Indian Ocean security

The annual summit between India and Japan saw the signing of key defense agreements and the official start of negotiations between the two countries on the acquisition and cross-service agreement (ACSA), which will grant reciprocal access to the bases and military facilities of each of their armed forces. A move to contain the rise of China and its aggressive posture in the Indian Ocean and other maritime areas.

Pm's balancing act in south Asian nations

India's relationship with its neighbors in South Asia was not in the most deniable place. But in India's favor, some changes and domestic political developments in the neighborhood have worked. The open interference of the missing Indians was also a welcome sign: The change of regime in the Maldives, the stable Nepal government and the visit of Modi sending the right signals, Sri Lanka overcoming an enormous political turmoil and showing strength in the elected representatives; they are a sign of the possibility of a greater commitment to India in South Asia.

Balancing ties with Israel & Palestine

When Prime Minister Narendra Modi landed in Ramallah on 10 February for a day's visit, it was a sign of solidarity with the Palestinian people and a commitment to "strengthening ties." The message from India was clear. In delicate relations with Israel and Palestine, India tried to maintain a balance. The dehyphenation policy of the two nations was seen positively in Ramallah because Palestine is no longer considered a "tail" of Israel, in which the main visit is to the latter and the former only receives a visit of courtesy.

For India, Israel is a strategic partner, and so Tel Aviv has always tried to push India away from Ramallah, leading to the initial vote of Modi's government against the Palestinian State at the UN, but the shift towards rebalancing ties with Palestine was evident when India's stakes in West Asia were realized in New Delhi, and India's partisan behavior hurt ties with other Muslims.

India and global solar alliance

India, together with France, took the lead of the International Solar Alliance when the world's so-called superpowers shied away from the planet's greatest challenge, global warming and climate change. India has deliberately worked on the issue of global climate problems

Us vs Iran: India holds its ground

India has not slipped or succumbed to pressure from the US on Iran. It succeeded in obtaining the US Waiver For Chabahar port, since it would connect India to Afghanistan via Iran and give countries stationed there an alternative to the Pakistan route, although it is clear from the point of view of oil imports that imports will have to be reduced to zero and oil imports have been significantly reduced. Iran has now come down to sixth place from the second largest oil exporter to India.

Grey-listing of Pak on terror

In order to ensure that the numbers swung against Pakistan and the global financial watchdog FATF placed Pakistan on its "grey list" during a plenary session in Paris, it took some hard diplomacy and smart negotiations, arguing that Pak did not act on terror financing. While the decision was taken in February this year to put Pakistan on the list, Islamabad was asked to submit an action plan to curb the financing of terrorism and counter-terrorism efforts. Pakistan launched a diplomatic attack in its 26-point action plan to avoid the "gray listing," but in vain. At each meeting of the FATF, the Indian delegation tried to prove the link between Pakistan's financial systems that promote and support terrorism.

Expectations from 2019:

If the US pulls soldiers out of Afghanistan, India will have a huge impact. Crown Prince Mohammad Bin Salman Al Saud from Saudi Arabia visits India. India-UAE-Saudi Arabia: India focuses on the extension of West Asia. Given the neighborhood, India will continue to reach South Asia. The Cold War between the US and China and Russia will have an impact on India.

Elections are closely monitored in countries such as Indonesia, Australia, Bangladesh. Any change in the guard, particularly in Bangladesh that goes to polls on 30 December, can change the region's dynamics.

UK-Brexit: On 29 March 2019, the UK is due to leave the EU. India is preparing to work with the UK, regardless of what happens next year since British Prime Minister Theresa May faces many challenges back home.

Challenges facing the government:

Pakistan

Pakistan was more an irritant than a challenge. With no relief from Pakistan's terrorism and the establishment raising the Kashmir issue to foster trouble in the valley, the message is clear that Pakistan's ISI and the new government of Imran Khan are only talking about peace, but they do not want better relations with India.

Terrorism

One of India's biggest challenges was cross-border terrorism. An area that India has used diplomatic means to tackle by ensuring that countries call out terrorist-harboring countries. The Khalistani movement is also gaining momentum in various countries through Pakistani agencies. The Kartarpur corridor is also seen as a gateway to abuse and create trouble in India by the Khalistanis. India has worked closely with countries with a large Sikh population.

Indo-US trade

Trade negotiations with the US remain a challenge. The' Trade Package' has yet to be developed by both sides.

CAATSA

India is still not clear when it comes to obtaining US waivers for many of the deals and defense equipment that India intends to purchase from countries such as Russia, such as the S-400s.

Chinese expansionism

China's expansionism, its continued support for Pakistan and India's cancelation of the Dalai Lama's birthday celebration in New Delhi, shows that Beijing is a work in progress despite the peace openings.

Modi's approach to China and Pakistan

The government of Narendra Modi has made India's neighborhood its top priority in foreign policy. Modi's first official foreign trip was to neighbor Bhutan, and he visited all of India's immediate neighbors in just over a year, with the exception of Pakistan and the Maldives (where a planned visit was suddenly canceled because of political differences). In an unprecedented move, he invited the seven other leaders of the South Asian Association for Regional Cooperation (SAARC), together with Mauritius, to his swearing-in ceremony in May 2014, and held his first set of meetings with them the following day, including Pakistani Prime Minister Nawaz Sharif. At the end of 2016, he is due to visit Pakistan for the SAARC summit, which will be the first Indian Prime Minister's visit to the country in more than a decade.

The neighborhood's primacy for Modi is clear. Unlike previous leaders, he is anxious to use foreign policy as a means of generating domestic growth and development inward investment, business and technology. As a pragmatist, he knows that strengthening regional cooperation and stability in South Asia will facilitate this. But it will be a difficult and complex task, especially given India's two powerful nuclear-armed neighbors, Pakistan and China, whose relations with India are marked by tensions and political and military standoffs. During his first year in office, Modi's policy towards both countries has undergone significant changes.

A tougher position on Pakistan

India and Pakistan have fought three wars over Kashmir and one over Bangladesh since independence almost 70 years ago. Once nuclear weapons were acquired in 1998, they shifted to military confrontations of lower intensity. Modi inherited difficult relations with Pakistan after his predecessor suspended bilateral peace talks due to an outbreak of violence and Pakistan's firing across the control line (loc), which divided the disputed Kashmir region.

The main threat from Pakistan to the Indian security establishment is another spectacular terrorist attack, such as the 2008 Mumbai attack, which could be carried out by militant groups based in Pakistan, such as Lashkar-e-Taiba (let) or Jaish-e-Mohammad (jem). The Indian security institution believes that any such attack would likely be planned and coordinated by elements of the Pakistani security institution, in particular its powerful intelligence organization, the Inter-Services Intelligence (ISI), which the Indian government has publicly accused of complicity in past terrorist attacks. New Delhi dismisses any suggestion of a "rogue" element in the ISI responsible for these incidents, or the ISI chief's lack of authorisation.

Modi has hardened India's position in relation to Pakistan. In August 2014, he canceled scheduled talks at the level of foreign secretaries on a meeting between Pakistan's high commissioner in India and the separatist group Hurriyat in Kashmir. At the SAARC summit in Kathmandu in November 2014, Modi and Sharif had a distinct chill. Then, in August 2015, India made it clear that it would not be acceptable for the Pakistani national security adviser to meet the leadership of Hurriyat or discuss anything other than terrorism, leading to the cancelation of the scheduled talks between the national security advisers of the two countries hours before the start of the talks. India also deliberately intensified its fire across the border and across the international border.

This hardline approach did not yield the Indian government's expected dividends. The Pakistani government refused to speed up the trial of seven alleged co-conspirators in the 2008 Mumbai terror attack, a key Indian demand, in a sign of defiance. A Pakistani court released the man accused of masterminding the attacks on bail in April 2015, after six years in prison, let operations chief Zakiur-Rehman Lakhvi. The conference of Pakistani corps commanders formally accused India's external intelligence agency, the Research and Analysis Wing (R&AW), for the first time in the following month of "whipping up terrorism" in Pakistan. It was believed that this accusation refers to repeated allegations of Indian involvement in terrorism in Baluchistan, Karachi and the tribal areas that India denied. The Indian Defense Minister later that month stated that "terrorists must be neutralized only by terrorists," leading his Pakistani counterpart to claim that this confirmed India's involvement in Pakistan's terrorism.

Pakistan has demonstrated a renewed will to counter terrorism since 143 school children and nine others were killed in Peshawar in December 2014 by the Tehreek-e-Taliban Pakistan (TTP)-Pakistan's Taliban branch. But this did not include terrorist groups against India. For example, the jem continues to operate banned militant outfit and address public rallies. No attempt was made to ban Jamaat-ud-Dawa (judge), a group considered a front for the outlawed letter and led by Chief Hafiz Saeed, on the grounds that there is no evidence to link the group with terrorism or letters. A formal proposal to ban the terrorist network of Haqqani is being considered.

India has a dilemma: It deals with the civil government of Pakistan, but it refuses to deal with the most powerful Pakistani institution in setting India policy -the army. There are no talks between the army and the army between the two countries. There are questions as to whether such talks would make sense for the Indian army, which has far less influence on policy than its counterpart, and whether the Pakistan army would even be inclined to talk to India, given that its raison d'être is a perceived existential threat from its neighbour.

To achieve regional cooperation with Pakistan in preparation for the 2016 SAARC summit, Modi needs to think "outside the box." Instead of simply seeking to strengthen the civilian government of Pakistan, he may need to engage with the Pakistani army and find out what India wants. This could begin with initial exchanges between the R&AW and the ISI, which participate in the annual meetings of the International Institute for Strategic Studies (IISS) on the security of South Asia in Oman and Bahrain in a unique way.

A robust China policy

China poses a strategic challenge rather than a threat to the Indian security establishment. India is primarily concerned about China's assertiveness in the border dispute, its growing trade and defense relations with India's neighbors in South Asia, and the expansion of Chinese influence in the Indian Ocean, which India is afraid of as much encirclement as possible. All of this has hardened New Delhi's view of Beijing. But China is India's biggest trading partner at the same time.

Despite seeking stronger trade and investment links with China, Modi has also been tough on his powerful neighbour. He criticized China's "mindset of expansion" in his election campaign. Indeed, at Modi's swearing-in ceremony, Tibet's exile Prime Minister Lobsang Sangay found himself in the official photograph. When Chinese forces crossed the Chumar Line of Actual Control (LAC) during President Xi Jinping's trip to India in September 2014, Modi's response was strong. He sent the area strengthenings and ensured that Indian troops held their positions. He expressed public concern about the border dispute and raised with his guest the issue of Beijing's neighborhood policies.

In contrast to a similar statement eight months earlier, the joint statement issued at the end of Modi's visit to China in May 2015 did not refer to maritime cooperation or Asia-Pacific security. Nor did it refer to China's One Belt, One Road initiative, or its Maritime Silk Road, which India suspiciously regards. India stated in June 2015 that the China-Pakistan Economic Corridor (CPEC) project was "not acceptable," as it would use infrastructure in the disputed territory of Kashmir.

A combined front with the US

Modi is prepared to form a combined front on Asia-Pacific security with the United States in a significant departure from the previous government to counter an assertive China. The two governments issued a document during President Barack Obama's visit to New Delhi in January 2015, which outlined their joint strategic vision for the

Asia-Pacific and Indian Ocean regions. It included a paragraph stating "the importance of safeguarding maritime security and ensuring freedom of navigation and flight throughout the region, in particular in the South China Sea" (emphasis added). This implied that the two parties had reached a consensus on the need to counter the assertive handling of conflicting regional territorial claims by Beijing. A 10-year framework agreement on defense was also signed with the United States, and trilateral cooperation between the United States, Japan and India was raised to the level of foreign secretary. The annual naval exercise between India and the United States Malabar has been expanded to include Japan. India is also seeking to strengthen Vietnam's defense and naval cooperation.

The joint vision between India and the United States recognizes the complementary nature of India's new "Act East" policy, which focuses on Japan and Australia, and the "pivot" or "rebalancing" of the Obama administration towards Asia. However, the extent to which the combined front between India, the United States and other democracies in the region, such as Australia and Japan, can go is limited. The quadrilateral naval exercise between Australia, India, Japan and the US, for example, has not been repeated in the last seven years after the first was followed by a stiff Chinese approach. The bottom line is that, while India and the US have an emerging bilateral consensus on security in the Asia-Pacific, they do not want a relationship of confrontation with China either.

Modi and Netanyahu are redefining 'security first'

The approach of vibrant democracies such as India and Israel to "security first" is fundamentally different from their non-democratic neighbours, who focused their actions on the enrichment of military power and the conception of world domination. In the case of India and Israel, the idea of "security first" is rooted in their traditional philosophy, which advocates strong defense and readiness to deal with any kind of threat, but at the same time is aligned with the changing realities of the time. Today, a country's security depends primarily on its economic and diplomatic strength. Prime Ministers Narendra Modi and Benjamin Netanyahu recognized and acted much earlier than others on this changing reality. Both leaders have redefined their country's traditional "security first" approach and everyone can see its results. "The combination of India's security and economic strengths will increase Israel's status as an asset in the eyes of other countries and thus increase India's diplomatic strength," Netanyahu said last August, while presenting his security cabinet with the "2030 security concept." Throughout his tenure, Netanyahu devoted his efforts not only to building strong military and intelligence capabilities.

Under Benjamin Netanyahu's leadership, the change in Israel's global image from a conflict zone to a start-up nation took place. Not only has he restored Israel's traditional diplomatic "security first" approach, he has expanded its scope to include economic power, which is also crucial to Israel's global standing. Earlier, there was an image that Israel reaches out to the world only for its strategic needs, which was required at that time, but today Israel reaches out to the world to offer its innovation and technological assets, and the world has begun to look more seriously than before at its national and security needs. This is a major change brought about by this Israeli administration! The transition in Israeli-Arab relations is also one of the diplomatic successes of the Netanyahu administration. As Israeli National Security Council's former head, Maj.-Gen. In an interview last year, Uzi Dayan said, "We can continue to build a vibrant Jewish and democratic state while offering the people around us our expertise. If we do this, many of our former enemies will eventually say that we want to do what you do for yours for our people.

On 29 September 2016, the Indian Army carried out surgical strikes across the control line in pok (Pakistan-Occupied Kashmir) and showed the world that India, which always exercises restraint, can also show power when necessary. The Indian government has established a strategic planning group to assist the country's National Security Council. The SPG consists of the National Security Adviser, the heads of all three defense services, the governor of the Reserve Bank of India, the vice-chairman of NITI Aayog (National Institution for the Transformation of India, the Indian Government's policy think tank), the cabinet secretary, the Foreign Secretary, the Home Secretary, the Finance Secretary and the Defense Secretary, as well as other key Defense, Energy, Energy and Energy bureaucrats.

Modi has taken an enormous step towards putting an end to India's silo-based security approach, which caused a delay in decision-making on key national security issues. India will also release its first strategy for national security. The Indian government set up a defense planning committee on April to prepare the draft national security strategy and facilitate comprehensive planning for defense forces. Modi has earned enormous appreciation worldwide for its economic reforms and foreign policy approach in a short span of four and a half years. Modi solves some of the decades-old problems of insurgency and left-wing extremism in the country's key Border States by combining an iron-fist strategy to address internal/external security challenges, policy reforms and a development-focused approach.

A fragmented approach has often led to an extremist system. Both India and Israel needed a comprehensive approach to their security interests. A careful observation of the transformation journey of both countries shows that their leaders have a holistic vision of their country's security. Before 2014, it seemed like a joke to compare the approach of Indian and Israeli leadership to security, but things have changed a lot since 2014! Modi is from a party whose founding fathers have a completely different approach to national security than the Congress of Nehru (India's longest ruling party). Jawaharlal Nehru (India's first prime minister) believed that there was no need for armed forces in India.

On the other hand, Pandit Deendayal Upadhyaya, the BJP's ideological guide (the current ruling party in India), subscribed to the doctrine that strike readiness is the best defense policy. He was a strong supporter of every individual's readiness to defend the nation and a strong advocate of the country's youth's compulsory military training. In defense and modernization of armed and police forces, he strongly advocated the adoption of advanced technologies. Inspired by Upadhyaya's core philosophy, Modi created a holistic vision for the country's security. During his first tenure, Modi launched extensive plans to modernize the military, modernize the police force and manage the border. There is also visible optimism in the country's ecosystem of defense and security. The government reaches out to the defense industry, msmes/startups and facilitates their participation in the defense supply chain through various creative media and platforms for the first time.

When it comes to security, both Modi and Netanyahu's actions are not limited to merely institutional improvements, they both understand how to develop a sustainable system through ideas, which can be brought forward in the future, as institutions are finite, but ideas are not! It would be an injustice to look at the relationship between India and Israel today in the light of a mere 'buyer-seller' perspective. This partnership's potential is huge! Both countries have a similar vision of "security first" and this truth is a solid foundation for future commitment.

CHAPTER FIVE

Modi Vs Monmohan

About Manmohan Singh

Singh, Manmohan

(born 26 September 1932, Gah, West Punjab, India[now in Pakistan]), an Indian economist and politician, who served from 2004 to 2014 as India's prime minister. He was the first non-Hindu to take over the office.

Singh attended Chandigarh Panjab University and Great Britain's Cambridge University. He later received a PhD in economics from Oxford University. He was appointed to a series of economic advisory positions with the Indian government in the 1970s and became a frequent consultant to prime ministers. Singh also served as director (1976-80) and governor (1982-85) at the Reserve Bank of India. The country was on the verge of an economic collapse when he was appointed finance minister in 1991. Singh devalued the rupee, reduced taxes, privatized state-run industries and encouraged foreign investment, reforms that helped transform the country's economy and boom the economy. He joined the Rajya Sabha (upper chamber of parliament) as a member of the Indian National Congress in 1991. Singh, who served as finance minister until 1996, ran in 1999 for Lok Sabha, but was defeated.

Congress won the parliamentary elections in May 2004 and defeated the ruling Bharatiya Janata Party (BJP). The leader of the Congress, Sonia Gandhi (widow of former Prime Minister Rajiv Gandhi), declined the prime ministry and recommended Singh for the post. Singh later formed a government and took office. His stated objectives included improving conditions for the poor in India (who generally did not benefit from the country's economic growth), ensuring peace with neighboring Pakistan and improving relations between the various religious groups in India.

Singh presided over a rapidly expanding economy, but rising fuel costs precipitated a marked increase in inflation, which threatened the ability of the government to provide subsidies to the poor of the country. Singh entered into negotiations with the United States in 2005 in an effort to meet India's growing energy demands. President George W. Bush for a pact for nuclear cooperation. The deal called for India to receive nuclear fuel technology and to be able to buy nuclear fuel on the world market. Abroad, those who were upset about India's refusal to sign the Nuclear Weapons Non-Proliferation Treaty resisted the prospective cooperation agreement; in India, Singh was criticized for fostering too close relations with the United States, which, according to his critics, would use the deal to leverage power in the Indian government. By 2008, progress in the deal prompted members of the parliamentary majority of the government-in particular communist parties-to denounce the government of Singh and ultimately push for a vote of confidence in Parliament at the end of July 2008. Singh's government narrowly survived the vote, but allegations of corruption and the purchase of votes on both sides marred the process.

Congress increased its number of seats in the legislature in the May 2009 parliamentary elections, and Singh took office as prime minister for the second time. However, a slowdown in India's economic growth and further allegations of corruption against officials of the Congress Party hampered governance during the second term of Singh and led to a deterioration in the popularity of the party with the electorate. Singh announced early in 2014 that he would not be seeking a third term as prime minister in the Lok Sabha election that spring. He left office on May 26, the same day the BJP was sworn in as prime minister by Narendra Modiof.

The Manmohan Singh Administration

India's 86-year-old prime minister, Manmohan Singh, is reluctant to meet the press. He has participated in only three official interactions with reporters in the decade since he entered India's highest political office. The last of these occurred on Friday, when Singh, close to the end of his second term, announced that he would not seek a third later that year in the general election. In a sense, the press conference was a late admission of Singh's political lame-duckhood, which began long before he revealed his intention to retire.

Installed as a placeholder for her son, Rahul, in 2004 by Sonia Gandhi, the reigning head of the Nehru-Gandhi family, Singh never really commanded his cabinet's obedience. "she's the queen," said Sonia, the party boss, a senior member of the Congress Party, as Singh was sworn in. "she appoints a regent to run some of the government's affairs. This arrangement, by which Singh would steer the economy while Sonia handled the messy business of politics, was intended to put India on a steady path of progress. Instead, it reduced the authority of the prime minister, created insubordination within the cabinet, and inaugurated an era of nearly insondable levels of corruption.

Graft has a history of hoarying in India. As early as 1964, just 17 years into India's independence, the Ministry of Home Affairs reported that corruption had "increased to such an extent that people began to lose faith in the integrity of the public administration." Corruption has become a daily fact of life in the decades since: There are few transactions in an ordinary citizen's interaction with the state that are not accompanied by the government. India's command economy inspired by the Soviet served as a catalyst for malfeasance in high offices in the state. It created a patronage culture in which senior politicians and bureaucrats showered favored people with lucrative business licenses.

But the time scams seem nearly trivial compared to the scandals that erupted on Singh's watch. One senior politician, Suresh Kalmadi, was placed in court in the notorious Tihar prison in Delhi on charges of pocketing millions in the run-up to the 2010 Commonwealth Games. Another prisoner in the same prison is former Communications Minister Andimuthu Raja, who is accused of defrauding the $40 billion national treasury by selling bandwidth at grossly underestimated rates. Singh now has the distinction of presiding over the most corrupt cabinet in Indian history, having scrupulously built up a cast-iron reputation for incorruptibility. The tragedy of Singh seems almost karmic when you think that the avarice that characterizes India today would be unthinkable without the policies he championed two decades ago.

India was a nation of 843 million citizens and five million telephone lines when Singh was a little-known civil servant in charge of the university grants commission in 1991. He was separated from bankruptcy by a billion dollars. Rarely did the Indian map look so vulnerable to another cartographic revision. If the flames of separatism seemed to be simmering in Punjab, the secessionist struggle in Kashmir peaked. Hindu nationalists, a fringe force in Indian politics just a decade ago, now occupied most of the seats of the opposition in parliament, ready to banish the laicism that was the foundation of Indian nationalism. India's guardian and lodestar, the U.S.S.R., lurched toward disintegration beyond its own imperiled borders. Moscow protected India from international criticism for its repression in Kashmir, maintained a crucial trade relationship of $6 billion and supplied defense equipment in exchange for goods. For a generation of Indians, the demise of the Soviet Union changed life's certainties. When Ved Mehta visited India at the time, he felt "a sense of fear about the country's economic, political and religious direction that I don't remember meeting in any of my other visits in the last 25 years."

The stubborn rhetoric of economic self-confidence and political non-alignment could no longer hide the deep decline of India. Here was a colossus of a country that forced its entrepreneurial citizens to make 50 trips to New Delhi and wait three years to import a computer, and where a telephone connection could take up to three years, the production of vacuum cleaners required a license, and Coca-Cola consumption was a criminal offence. Induced into the cabinet for his economic expertise as finance minister, Singh urged the government to devalue the rupee and adopt austerity. He drew up a plan that would substantially deregulate industry, delicate the private sector, remove barriers to foreign investment, grant tax concessions to private companies, cut subsidies to farmers and curb labor activism.

The plan was so radical that Singh's own party, Congress, stood up against it. The Herald, the party's newspaper, said that its policy was designed to give "the Indian middle-class crispier cornflakes [and] fizzier aerated drinks." "That," the paper affirmed, "could never have been the vision of the founding fathers of our nation."

But the policies of Singh seemed to bear fruit. India attracted more foreign investment by the end of 1995 than it had managed combined in the previous four decades. Two-way trade with the United States alone grew to $7.3 billion. With investments in India, there were 422 American companies. In and out of the country, Ceos of major companies streamed. After 20 years, Coca-Cola was back on the subcontinent. The socialist George Fernandes, who banned Coca-Cola in 1977, stood in parliament and asked Singh for an answer. "do we need Coke? Need we Pepsi? "

But India was starting to look like another country by then. The middle class has become more conspicuous than ever. Indians now drank 2.880 million bottles of fizzy drinks between them and flew 10 million miles annually. By 1996, the credit card industry, which had barely had a presence in India before the economic reforms of Singh, expanded into a $64 million business. In India alone, Mastercard grew 106 percent -the highest growth ever recorded in Asia. The creed of this emerging "New India" was captured on the billboards of major cities in the advertising slogans:

"I. I'm. "Mine," "It's My Life," "Keep Up Or Be Left Out," "Zamana Badal Gaya Hai: Times Have Changed." The Economic Times, an early supporter of Singh's reforms, saw its circulation exceed 500,000 of less than 100,000 just four years ago, making it the world's second largest business paper. "One of the psychological legacies of the... socialist era was that the more affluent sections of society were branded rather vulgar and it was considered an even greater sin to spend money to live well," one commentator wrote. "this stigma seems to have disappeared for many today."

This was a jubilant and hopeful place for Singh's India. But there was another India far from it. In a report released by Oxfam, his harrowing realities were captured. Rural poverty grew from 33 percent to 48 percent in the reform years, and the poorest bore a disproportionate burden on Singh's deficit reduction program. Since tax concessions from the government to the private sector made it impossible to increase revenue, public investment and social expenditure were reduced. At the same time, more than a dozen of the top 50 private companies in the country have been able to completely avoid taxes.

It remains a matter of dispute whether Singh's reforms helped or hurt India. But this is clear: Singh was an economist, not a politician, and the policies he advocated were only implemented because someone else was willing to bear the political costs. Congress suffered the worst defeat in its history in the subsequent general elections. When the party came back to power in 2004, Singh was still an apolitical figure who had never won an election in his life, despite his experience in government. The Italian origin of Sonia Gandhi threatened to grist the xenophobic opposition. So she went to Singh. Singh has since mumbled inaudibly, knowing power only as a gift, not as a responsibility. His admirers have long argued that Singh is indifferent to power, even if he brings some dignity to the prime minister's office. The opposite is true: One must desperately love power to accept a job just to be close to it.

The greatest achievement in Singh's office, the only act that can be described as affirmative, was the civil nuclear agreement he negotiated with the United States. His most persistent failure must be to deal with Mumbai's terrorist siege in 2008. Singh actually moved India closer than ever to a conflict with Pakistan by avoiding confrontation with Pakistan for fear of inciting a war. Where Indians once wanted to ignore the most serious acts of terror, even the slightest transgression today provokes a cry for war. If Singh had shown determination and forced Pakistan to extradite the men who masterminded the attacks in India, the appeal of India's hardliners would have been diminished. There has been tremendous sympathy for India's cause throughout the world. Singh didn't capitalize on it. Singh's self-injured "peace initiative" with Pakistan is the only beneficiary of Hindu nationalists in India and Muslim militants in Pakistan.

Consider New Delhi's view as Singh is about to leave the office. Maoist insurgents control significant parts of rural India. Rural India continues to be a very violent place. Urban India is a hideous inequality theater. In the east, the Chinese army continues to invade Indian territory on a regular basis. The men who masterminded the attack on Mumbai in the west remain in freedom. Even India's relationship with the U.S., which Singh so highly prized, has deteriorated abruptly over the past month. Hindu nationalists are ready to take power at home in Delhi. "History will kindly judge me," Singh said Friday. Indians are also a notoriously ahistorical people. To be forgotten is the best Singh can hope for.

Manmohan Singh and Modi's Administration

It is a rare occasion for former PM Manmohan Singh to take part in a debate in Parliament. To criticize the government's implementation of the demonization drive. And in order to demolish the arguments of the treasury banks ' drive to benefit the county in the long run, he quoted a half quote from British economist John Maynard Keynes: "In the long run, we're all dead." During the debate, he may have cited Keynes out of context. Ironically, India needs demonetisation because Singh failed to implement the theory of Keynes as PM. And he couldn't control the side effects of corruption, nepotism and public expenditure misuse.

In 2008, in the midst of a global recession, Singh decided to push banks-mainly public-sector banks-to lend in the critical five sectors of civil aviation, power, road, steel and urban infrastructure to stimulate growth in India. We all saw these sectors break down by 2011. The much-hyped umpps and investments in power generation have declined, airlines and companies investing in civil aviation have not seen a future, investors in the road sector have nearly failed, and their investments have declined. This also led to nepotism, corruption and public money abuse. The result was black money generation and banks' npas.

In his book-A Monetary Reform Treaty-the British economist used this quote to criticize the measures taken by the then British government to deal with the Great Depression and advocated more public expenditure to stimulate demand. Keynes thought fiscal deficits in government budgets were not bad all his life. That government borrowing of one kind or another is, so to speak, the remedy of nature to prevent business losses from falling into such a severe slump as the present one (the Great Depression), so great that production is completely stopped. And that might not lead to inflation.

Singh saw the theory's merits in bringing the world out of recession. And at the 2008 G20 summit in Washington, where he advocated Keynes' stimulus to the world to emerge from the great recession, he was famous. In the five critical sectors, he pushed the public banks back home to lend. He also paved the way for schemes such as MGNREGA, food right, etc.

But Keynes's irony is that he only succeeded in bringing the economies of the western world out of the tremor of the Second World War, never after. By the way, many of the mixed economies initially followed the principles of leaving the public sector and faced similar "side effects" challenges. This includes, inter alia, China, Russia. The leadership test remains to check the side effects. But in India, because of inefficient political leadership, things went out of control. In 1977, the British rejected the theory and moved away, despite the era known as capitalism's golden age, but the side effects became too great to handle.

So in 2016 it's for India. By the time Singh retired from office in 2014, all five sectors were bust, and many of the projects in these sectors turned npas for banks, mainly public-sector banks, bleeding corporate-house balance sheets. This began during the tenure of Singh. The NPA numbers were Rs 66,686 crore in September 2009, which rose to Rs 2,40,947 crore when he left office, and the effect of the snowball only worsens the numbers. Keynes stimuli have also not worked globally, either in the United States or in Europe. But it has led to a short-term and long-term respite in inflation, "artificial" profit booking, and black economy creation and de-growth job creation.

About Narendra Modi

PM Narendra Modi

Narendra Modi, Narendra Damodardas Modi (born September 17, 1950, Vadnagar, India), Indian politician and government official, who became the leader of the Bharatiya Janata Party (BJP). In 2014, he led his party to victory in elections to the Indian Parliament's Lok Sabha (lower chamber), after which he was sworn in as India's prime minister. Prior to that, he served as chief minister (head of government) of the state of Gujarat in western India (2001-14).

Early Life And Political Career

In a small town in northern Gujarat, Modi was raised and completed an M.A. Graduated from Gujarat University in Ahmadabad in political science. In the early 1970s, he joined the pro-Hindu organization Rashtriya Swayamsevak Sangh (RSS) and set up an RSS student wing unit in his area, Akhil Bharatiya Vidyarthi Parishad. Modi steadily rose in the hierarchy of the RSS and his association with the organization benefited greatly from his subsequent political career.

Modi joined the BJP in 1987, and a year later he became secretary-general of the party's Gujarat branch. He played an important role in strengthening the party's presence in the state in the years to come. In 1990, Modi was one of the members of the BJP who took part in a state coalition government, and he helped the BJP succeed in the 1995 elections to the state legislative assembly, which in March allowed the party to form the first government in India controlled by the BJP. The state government's control by the BJP was relatively short-lived, but it ended in September 1996.

Political Ascent And Term As Chief Minister Of Gujarat

In 1995 Modi was appointed secretary of the national organization of the BJP in New Delhi, and three years later he was appointed secretary general. He remained for another three years in that office, but in October 2001 he replaced the incumbent chief minister of Gujarat, fellow BJP member Keshubhai Patel, after Patel was held responsible for the poor response of the state government following the massive earthquake in Gujarat earlier that year, which killed more than 20,000 people. In a by-election in February 2002 that won him a seat in the Gujarat state assembly, Modi entered his first ever election contest.

The political career of Modi subsequently remained a mix of deep controversy and self-promoted achievements. His role as chief minister was particularly questioned during the communal riots in Gujarat in 2002. He was accused of condoning the violence, or at least of doing little to stop the killing of more than 1,000 people, mostly Muslims, following the deaths of dozens of Hindu passengers when their trains were set on fire in Godhra City. The United States refused to grant him a diplomatic visa in 2005 on the grounds that he was responsible for the riots in 2002, and the United Kingdom also criticized his role in 2002. Although Modi himself escaped any accusation or censure-either by the judiciary or by investigative agencies-in the years that followed, some of his close associates were found guilty of complicity in the events of 2002 and were sentenced to long imprisonment. The administration of Modi was also accused by police or other authorities of involvement in extrajudicial killings (variously referred to as "encounters" or "false encounters." One such case in 2004 involved the death of a woman and three men whose officials said they were members of Lashkar-e-Taiba (a terrorist organization based in Pakistan involved in the Mumbai terrorist attacks in 2008) and allegedly conspired to murder Modi.

However, Modi's repeated political success in Gujarat made him an indispensable leader in the BJP hierarchy and led to his reintegration into the mainstream of politics. Under his leadership, the BJP achieved a significant victory in the parliamentary elections in December 2002, winning 127 of the 182 seats in the chamber (including Modi's seat). The BJP, which projected a manifesto for growth and development in Gujarat, was again victorious in the 2007 elections to the state assembly, with a total of 117 seats, and the party again prevailed in the 2012 polls, with 115 seats. Modi won his contests both times and came back as chief minister.

During his time as head of the government in Gujarat, Modi established a tremendous reputation as a capable administrator and was credited with the rapid growth of the state's economy. In addition, his electoral performance and that of the party helped to advance Modi's position as not only the party's most influential leader, but also a potential candidate for India's prime minister. In June 2013, Modi was selected as the BJP's campaign leader for the Lok Sabha 2014 election.

The struggles of PM Narendra Modi

Your attitude is said to be your altitude; it determines how high you are flying. A little boy from Vadnagar, India, understood this simple yet crucial statement well. Just three years after India became independent of the British Raj, in September 1950, Narendra, the son of Darmodradas Modi and Hiraba Modi, was born into a family born into a family that had to fight hard to meet the ends. Narendra's hometown was Vadnagar in Gujarat's Mehsana district, the place once visited by the famous Chinese traveler Hiuen Tsang and a place known for its spirituality and learning richness. Narendra, the third of the Modis' six children, began to dream of a life where he could wipe the tears of the suffering people and make a big difference to their lives in their small single-story house.

Little Narendra also helped his father sell tea at the local railway station in Vadnagar in his tea stall. Modi used to spend hours in his school library as an ardent lover and debater. He had friends from various communities and celebrated with the same zeal both Hindus and Muslim festivals. Modi was only eight years old when he introduced himself to the Rashtriya Swayamsevak Sangh (RSS) and met Lakshmanrao Inamdar, known as his political guru and mentor.

His parents, following their family tradition, engaged him to Jashodaben Chimanlal when he was only 13. But Narendra, known as' balswayamsevak' or a junior cadet in RSS, had already given political heart. So even after he married Jashodaben before he was eighteen, Narendra was unable to pursue his marital life and left home to chase his dreams. For Narendra Modi, it was a remarkable journey. Narendra was only 9 years old when the Tapi River was created by a massive flood. This little boy took a step forward and with his friends set up a food stall. All the proceeds for the relief work were donated. His attempt at serving his mother India at this tender age was indeed remarkable, which silently laid the foundation for the establishment of a worthy nation's prime minister.

He left no unturned stone wondering one day to serve his nation. He also dreamed of joining the Indian Army, but his family's strong opposition never allowed him to make his dream come true. Modi was a powerful dreamer. He has always been guided by his Antyodaya principle or' serving the most distant.' When Keshubai Patel stepped down as Chief Minister of Gujarat in the wake of the earthquake in Kutch in January 2001 that killed thousands of people, Modi got his big break. Modi was then selected as Patel's replacement to become the longest-serving chief minister of Gujarat. And he has been ensuring steady GDP growth ever since. Indeed, under this development man, Gujarat has shown overall growth in agriculture, manufacturing and services. But riots broke out in February 2002 after 59 passengers, mainly Hindu pilgrims, died in Godhra train fire in Gujarat. At least 1,000 people died. Critics accused Chief Minister Modi of not doing enough to stem the riots and even quietly encourage them, allegations he strongly denied and that were never proven.

In 2013, Modi was chosen to lead the general election campaign of the BJP in 2014, making him the prime ministerial candidate of the party. But at the beginning, there were doubts as to whether Modi could attract allies to the charm of Atal Bihari Vajpayee, even considered moderate by his rivals. But the BJP put all its eggs in the Modi basket, a gamble that paid Modi to attract more pre-poll allies, including those who left the NDA to blame him for the riots in 2002. But his supporters see Modi as a "strong leader" who won't play any section's appeasement policy.

The world's leading financial newspaper, the Financial Times, praised the development of a decade in Gujarat under Modi's leadership, and in fact the most prestigious TIME magazine in the world featured him on its cover page. The United States Congress called him "the King of Governance." "Modi means business," Times Magazine said. Born in a backward community of' Modh Ghanchi' (oil crusher) in the historic Mehsana district of Vadnagar, Modi's rise is phenomenal. His status as a person belonging to the backward community was also contested, however.

Premiership

Following a vigorous campaign -in which Modi portrayed himself as a pragmatic candidate who could turn India's underperforming economy around -he and the party won, with the BJP gaining a clear majority of seats in the chamber. Modi was sworn in on May 26, 2014 as prime minister. Shortly after taking office, his government embarked on several reforms, including campaigns to improve India's transport infrastructure and liberalize the country's rules on foreign direct investment. Early in his term, Modi scored two major diplomatic achievements. He hosted a visit by Chinese President Xi Jinping in mid-

September, the first time in eight years that a Chinese leader was in India. At the end of that month, Modi made a highly successful visit to New York City, including a meeting with the United States, after being granted a U.S. visa. Pressure. Barack Barack Obama.

As prime minister, Modi was responsible for promoting Hindu culture and implementing economic reforms. The government took measures that would generally appeal to Hindus, such as its attempt to ban the sale of slaughtered cows. Economic reforms were widespread, introducing structural changes -and temporary disruptions -that could be felt throughout the country. The demonetization and replacement of 500-and 1,000-rupee banknotes with just a few hours ' notice was among the most far-reaching. The purpose was to stop "black money" by making it difficult to exchange large amounts of cash. The government centralized the consumption tax system in the following year by introducing the Goods and Services Tax (GST), which replaced a confusing system of local taxes on consumption and eliminated the problem of cascading tax. GDP growth slowed from these changes, although growth was already high (8.2% in 2015), and the government's tax base was expanded by the reforms.

UPA vs NDA Government: Comparison Since 2014 to2017

Today, India has been tagged as the world's fastest growing economy. The economy's size has grown to 2.54

lakh crores, making it the world's seventh largest economy. In this book, we compared changes in India's various economic sectors from 2014 to 2017. In this book, we basically compared the current NDA government's three years of resuming office in 2014 and the performance of the previous UPA government. In this book, we explained the changes in the Indian economy's various areas.

Let's have a look:

Size of Economy:

Top Ten Economies

Rank	Economic Freedom (Heritage Foundation)	Rank 2015 (out of 178)	Rank 2016 (out of 178)	Rank	GDP % Growth Forecast (IMF World Economic Outlook)	2017
1	United Kingdom	13	10	1	India	7.6
2	United States	12	11	2	China	6.2
3	Germany	16	17	3	United States	2.2
4	Japan	20	22	4	Germany	1.4
5	France	73	75	5	France	1.4
6	Italy	80	86	6	Russia	1.1
7	Brazil	118	122	7	United Kingdom	1
8	India	128	123	8	Italy	0.9
9	China	138	144	9	Japan	0.6
10	Russia	143	153	10	Brazil	0.4

Inflation Rate

(Wholesale Price Index -WPI):

In 2013-14: 5.2% (Base Year -2004-05)

In 2016-17: 1.7% (Base Year -2011-12)

Consumer Price Index-CPI:

In 2013-14 : 9.4% (Base Year -2004-05)

In 2016-17 : 4.5% (Base Year -2011-12)

Expenditure on Education

A. During the UPA government, education expenditure was Rs. 65,867 crore, which in 2017-18 increased to Rs. 79,868 crore under the NDA regime.

B. The number of total universities in the country during the UPA regime (2013-14) was 723, which increased to 799 in the NDA regime (2016-17), which means that 76 new universities were established during the NDA regime.

C. The total number of colleges in the country during the UPA (2013-14) amounted to 36,634, which increased to 39071 during the NDA regime (2016-17), i.e. 2437 new colleges were created.

D. The total number of schools in the country during the UPA (2013-14) was 1518160, which increased to 1522346 during the NDA reign, i.e. The total number of new schools has been added to 4186.

Tax Collection

The highest increase in income earned from excise duty was in the current tenure of the NDA government. This income in 2013-14 was Rs. 1.70 lakh crore, which increased by 139 percent during the NDA government's tenure of Rs. 4.06 lakh crore. During the total tax collection of the UPA government in 2013-14, 8.16 lakh crores increased to 12.27 lakh crores in the current government, i.e. a 50 percent increase. In 2016-17, property tax was abolished.

Expenditure on health:

The UPA government spent only 1.2% of GDP on health in 2013-14, which increased to 1.4% in 2016-17. The NDA Government provided Rs. 48,878 crore for the 2017-18 health sector, which in 2013-14 was Rs. 37,330 crore. In 2017, the current government declared a new national health policy aimed at increasing the average age from 67.5 years to 70 years by 2025, with a target of 2.5 percent of GDP in health care.

Agriculture Production:

The production of food grains in the country in 2013-14 was 2650 lakh tonnes, an estimated 273 lakh tonnes, in 2016-17. Growth in agriculture during the UPA regime was 4.01 percent, which increased in 2016-17 to 4.83 percent. This year, the NDA government targeted a loan of Rs 10 lakh crore to farmers, while a 7.11 lakh crore farm loan was distributed under the UPA regime.

Employment Generation

Almost 1.35 lakh jobs were created in the country in the 2015-16 financial year, while it was 4.20 lakh during the UPA regime. However, 2.13 lakh of new jobs were created in India in 2016-17, in which service, manufacturing and trade were the main contributing sectors. More than 30 percent of the country's young people aged 15 to 30 are currently unemployed or not in training. It can therefore be concluded that Modi Government's overall performance in terms of job generation does not match marks.

Housing for All

According to the 2011 Census data, the rented houses are home to 27 percent of people in cities. Under the housing scheme of the Prime Minister, 18 lakh houses were built while a total of 13.82 lakh houses were built during the tenure of 10 years during the UPA regime. For 2016-17, the current NDA government has allocated Rs. 15 lakh crore. It should be noted that India will need 30 million houses by 2022.

Industrial Development

In 2013-14, the industrial sector contributed 31.60 percent to the country's GDP, which is expected to fall to 31.12 percent in 2016-17. The industrial growth rate in the current NDA government is 4.5 percent, which is slightly better than the 4.2 percent of the previous UPA government. In 2013-14, 25.30 lakh cars were sold in India, while the figure in 2016-17 is 30.46 lakh in the current government.

Foreign Direct Investment

In 2013-14, the influx of foreign direct investment in India was $36 billion, which increased to $55 billion in 2016-17. The Modi government increased the FDI limit for cable and DTH services from 74 percent to 100 percent, while this limit for news channels and radio channels increased from 26 percent to 49 percent. It can now be concluded that the NDA government is performing better than the previous UPA government, which is why the Indian economy's economic prospects look very encouraging, with the exception of jobs. India has a very bright future ahead, as the Indian population is currently 55 percent below the 25 years that have made it the world's youngest economy.

Modi-fied India

That's why the whole world is looking to India for its young
talent.

CHAPTER SIX

The emergence of new India

Modi's government and structural reforms

Progress in reforms is like the hour-hand movement of the clock: The human eye cannot detect the movement in it, but it has gone full circle twice a day. While naysayers complain that reforms have not made progress, reforms have accumulated in the last four years to the point that only highlights can fit a newspaper column.

In the United Progressive Alliance (UPA) government's last two full fiscal years, inflation averaged 9.7 percent and growth was 5.9 percent. In order to tackle inflation, the new government adopted monetary-focused inflation and a strict fiscal consolidation plan. It has undertaken numerous structural reforms to address growth. In the last four years, the result was an average inflation rate of 4.3 percent and GDP growth of 7.3 percent.

Governance was the government's key focus. The concerted efforts of the government to improve business ease have resulted in India jumping from 140th to 100th place in the rankings of the World Bank. At the same time, the government has worked to make life easier. Citizens no longer need copies of degrees and diplomas certified by a Gazetted Officer; they can store soft copies of their degrees and diplomas in a digilocker, and they can access many central and state services online via the Umang portal. Under Ujjwala Yojana, 40 million BPL households have received LPG connections.

The government works to end war-based corruption. An integral part of this effort was demonization, an audacious act. It has yielded a beautiful dividend through many channels: The detection and closure of shell companies; the disqualification of company directors; the destruction of black real estate wealth by a sharp decline in prices; an increase in the number of income tax payers; and a strong signal of the government's determination to combat corruption. A major institutional innovation was the replacement of the Planning Commission by Niti Aayog. The new institution has emerged as an active promoter of the reform agenda of the prime minister. It has also established a more friendly and equal relationship with the states.

The second set of reforms demonstrates the government's ability to implement large-scale programs. Aadhaar, Jan Dhan Yojana (JDY) and Swachh Bharat Mission (SBM) are three initiatives in this category. Aadhaar cards rose from March 2014 to 1.2 billion from 650 million. In August 2017 alone, the government issued 8.65 million cards at the peak. Under JDY, in one week during August 23-29, 2014, 18 million bank accounts were opened, a feat mentioned in the Guinness Book of World Records.

Today, there are 316 million JDY accounts in total. Finally, rural households with toilets in their homes have risen from barely 38 percent to 84.2 percent under SBM, with 17 states declared free of open defecation in rural areas. We are now within walking distance of Mahatma Gandhi's 150th birth anniversary by October 2, 2019.

Important structural reforms include the deregulation of oil and diesel prices, the further opening up of foreign direct investment (FDI), the shift to direct transfers of benefits (DBT), the Goods and Services Tax (GST), the Insolvency and Bankruptcy Code (IBC), and academic and administrative autonomy to top universities and universities. On oil and diesel prices, despite political pressure from all sides, the government must be applauded for refusing to reverse the reform. The opening in the e-marketplace on FDI promises a major overhaul of India's retail marketing. The shift to DBT using Aadhaar instrumentality has led to the elimination of many beneficiaries of ghosts.

Despite the GST reform, which required a constitutional amendment and multiple laws, various criticisms of its implementation constitute a landmark achievement of the government. We can count on significant gains in efficiency with a single national tax replacing a large number of state and central taxes. The movement of commercial vehicles along roads has already accelerated by an average of 15 percent. For almost two decades, I have lamented that India lacks a modern bankruptcy law. This glaring gap was finally filled by IBC. On the basis of this, the circular of 12 February 2018 of the Reserve Bank of India (RBI) modernized regulations governing the recovery of bank loans. This reform will help to solve the recurring problem of non-performing assets (npas). RBI also successfully deploys IBC to clean up existing npas, as the case of Bhushan Steel shows.

Despite their launch almost three decades ago, the area of higher education was left untouched by reforms. This too has now been addressed by the government giving top universities and colleges unprecedented academic and administrative autonomy. The reform will foster much-needed competition between academic institutions. However, international trade is one area in which the government has erred. Decades of efforts by governments led by both BJP and Congress to liberalize trade have been reversed, with customs duties on a large number of products increasing. We also failed to forge free trade agreements with trading partners that opened up the market. In this important area, the next government will need to correct the course.

The many failures of Manmohan Singh

The Florentine political thinker Niccolo Machiavelli could well have written about Manmohan Singh when he briefly explained in the seventh chapter of The Prince, his classic treatise on the art of government, how weak rulers tend to be men who become princes either by luck or for the sake of others. Their effectiveness depends on their patron's benevolence rather than on their own political base: "These (leaders) stand on the goodwill and fortune of the one who raised them-two most unconstant and unstable things."

The controversial memoirs of Sanjaya Baru, the former prime minister's press adviser, confirm what many suspected: Real power did not reside with Singh, but with his political benefactor. The allegations that Sonia Gandhi had been shown key files before they reached Singh are one example of how constitutional proprietary was thrown into the wind. The shortcomings in the unique political deal that took Singh to the top position in 2004 became clear as the years passed. India had to pay a regime's price in contradiction to itself.

Singh should not be regarded as an innocent victim of the entropic process. He was a participant who was willing. His first address to the nation in May 2004 was in line with what he used to say as finance minister: that India should reform its economy in order to create the conditions for the kind of labor-intensive industrialization that has taken so many other Asian countries out of mass poverty. The government should use its growing tax revenue to build the necessary physical and social infrastructure to help citizens take advantage of growing opportunities. This vision quickly dissipated into the ether.

The first Singh government failed to pursue the economic reforms necessary to consolidate the economic progress record after 2003. It was lulled into believing that continued rapid growth was a birthright and agreed to frontload expenditure in the erroneous belief that tax revenue would follow. The second Singh government failed to withdraw the fiscal stimulus after the crisis, which hit India with high inflation at a time when the economy was losing momentum rapidly. Some of this excess demand spilled into the trade account so that India was dangerously close to a balance of payments mess once last year's possibility of global monetary tightening became clear. And it was bizarre for individual policy acts such as retrospective taxation.

An economist's failure to steer the economy is disconcerting. One common explanation is that Singh focused more on foreign policy in order to secure India's emerging position in the world and create his own broader political legacy. A less charitable explanation is that he preferred foreign policy because in foreign capitals he was treated with more respect than in New Delhi. The nuclear deal between the United States and India was definitely a feather in his cap. He had less success in reaching a meaningful peace deal with Pakistan, an objective close to his heart.

Singh recently said he hopes that history will judge him better than today's critics. As an economic administrator, his long service to the nation since joining the government four decades ago has had many highlights, in particular his role in the landmark economic reforms launched by the P.V government. Rao Narasimha. But what has happened in recent years will obscure his public record.

It was a paradox for Singh. He's an economist who has been watching the economy lose direction. He is an exemplary honest man who led one of Indian history's most corrupt governments. The very class that benefited richly from economic reforms has deserted him. One reason why so many Indians are now looking for a strong leader in Narendra Modi is his weakness. These are the dialectical truths to be dealt with by future historians.

Narendra Modi: transformative global leader

India has emerged as an international power through recent dramatic domestic economic reforms and the emergence of a stable majority government in recent elections, despite a multitude of political and business risks. The credit for this belongs to the dynamic leadership of Prime Minister Narendra Modi, who has taken bold steps in nearly four years to route corruption, formalize the economy and be rewarded by Indians in recent state elections with control of the Rajya Sabha (State Council).

Modi-fied India

Modi's India aspires to the status of great power and is clearly on the way to achieving this objective. The Modi Government has a clear view of its key geopolitical allies, including the United States, Russia, Japan and Canada, which are considered to have mutual interests with India. Since the beginning of his administration, Modi's leadership has been robust, focusing on changing the country's traditional non-alignment of the Cold War into a series of strategic alignments focused on the country's economic performance. These relationships can only be relied on to deepen under his leadership with historic strategic partnerships with the United States and Canada and major investment deals with Japan.

The vision and reform agenda of Modi is driven economically by what can be described as "perpetual action" and transformation. It is based on success. He was driven by his energetic reform agenda as Gujarat's chief minister to national leadership. We see him replicating this formula as Prime Minister: A handful of marquee reforms supplemented by a flurry of lower profile, more techno-conscious reforms.

Modi's most iconic reform to date has been the decision to "demonetize" the economy; withdrawing modest currency denominations, which can be replaced only by bank accounts with new bills. Designed as a program to remove India from a cash-based economy, Modi builds the foundations of an effective tax system, eliminates corruption and promotes long-term economic development. The Indian people, bold and controversial as the step towards demonetization was, endorsed Modi's plan with a historic and far-reaching victory in state elections, especially in Uttar Pradesh. The initiative and Modi's economic stewardship, having paid significant short-term costs to achieve this goal, in particular in the form of criticisms from the opposition and the media, won broad domestic support. The global business community should pay close attention to the serious changes taking place in India as the country becomes a more stable and attractive investment and operation market.

Less known, but equally important reforms include a national tax on goods and services, changes to the bankruptcy code and the start of a public service overhaul. In combination with major initiatives in education, infrastructure, trade and the formalization of the Indian economy, there are encouraging signs that traditional barriers to business are being replaced by growth accelerants.

Although this list can be expected to grow, India's historical institutions will try to impede the transformation rate. State-run banks hold large amounts of unsuccessful assets and can be counted on to erect local barriers. Similarly, since land reform is largely managed at state level, agricultural and industrial rezoning reforms will be slow. An administration emboldened to accelerate economic reform and industrial development will fiercely challenge this inertia.

The best prospects for India are long-term, as exciting as the next chapter is. The continued struck by endemic poverty, profound social divisions and complex politics - especially the extent to which these factors inhibited the emergence of the world's largest democracy as an economic powerhouse. Not since Indira Ghandi had the quality and strength of leadership displayed Narendra Modi. His recent success in the polls should not be underestimated; it is an Indian people's powerful mandate. The time has come to invest in India, best reserved for the knowledgeable and patient.

Dentons and Harper & Associates work together in a unique global affiliation to provide assessment services, entry strategies and opportunities to participate in this emerging powerhouse to customers interested in doing business in India. Harper & Associates work from the Dentons office in Calgary and works as a consultant with the worldwide team and customers of the company. Building on his international experience and network as a leader of the G-7, Mr. Harper provides customers with advice on market access, global geopolitical and economic risk management, and how to maximize value in global markets.

Scaling the 4 years of Modi government

The government of Narendra Modi has been in office for four years. During this period, several economic reforms have been carried out and a number of development programs have been launched -Pradhan Mantri Jan-Dhan Yojana, Digital India, Make-in-India, Skill India, Pradhan Mantri MUDRA Yojana, Swachh Bharat Abhiyan, Ayushman Bharat, etc. What is the meaning of a common man for the current government's various economic reforms and development programmes?

It offers a useful perspective to answer this question from the perspective of an economist. Economists tend to look at reforms/programs that (1) address market failures, (2) promote equity and reduce poverty and (3) address the failures of the government. Even the strongest market supporters recognize that the market mechanism breaks down and therefore justifies government intervention. Whether public goods such as large infrastructure projects or activities that have negative / positive spillover effects on the economy are supplied, government intervention is required. Similarly, to verify that companies use their dominant market positions or step in to fill "missing" markets, government intervention is required to correct these market failures. The government also has a role to play in providing macroeconomic stability.

Addressing market failures

The strong push by the Modi government to build infrastructure projects -not only for new projects, but also to kick-start previous governments' stalled projects -is well-meaning in that it addresses the failure of the public goods market.

Similarly, a strong push for digital transactions or the launch of Swachh Bharat is all about capturing the large positive spillovers in the development processes of each of these interventions. Similarly, advancing the implementation of emission standards at the Bharat stage from IV to VI to curb vehicle pollution or banning the sale and import of oxytocin to prevent its possible abuse means reducing negative spillovers.

The government is also filling in the "missing" markets by implementing programs such as Jan-Dhan for financial inclusion, Housing for All to subsidize the cost of home loans in order to make housing affordable for the poor, Skill India to provide vocational and technical training, and many more.

To maintain macroeconomic stability, economic growth is important. In order to boost sustainable economic growth, the government has launched various programs to increase agricultural production and productivity, including Pradhan Mantri Krishi Sinchayee Yojana, Soil Health Cards, Fasal Bima Yojana, etc., in order to encourage small businesses and innovators through easy bank financing (MUDRA Yojana, Start-Up India). Looking at the thrust of economic growth, the government seems to be seeking not only to diversify sources of growth, but also to democratize growth by unlocking the potential of people from all sections of society.

Promoting equity

The government has pursued initiatives specific to certain regions and certain population subgroups in order to promote equity. For example, it has placed particular emphasis on the development of the Northeast-the long-neglected region. Similarly, more than 100 "aspirational" districts have been identified, lagging behind certain key indicators of development. The government places special emphasis on accelerating the pace of development in these districts under its Aspirational District Transformation programme.

The government has launched several initiatives to promote equity among specific populations -free LPG (clean cooking fuel) connections to women from BPL families under Pradhan Mantri Ujjwala Yojana to protect their health, a national dialysis program aimed at providing free dialysis services to poor patients in more than 500 districts and so on.

Addressing government failures

One of the important functions of any government in a market economy is to set standards and develop regulations so that markets can work well. The government has, in fact, strengthened the regulatory role, as evidenced by the adoption of the Real Estate Act, in order to safeguard the interests of home buyers, strengthen food safety regulations, tighten banking regulations, etc. The government is also beginning to address regulatory issues in the social sector. For example, in the health sector, which is full of commissions and kickbacks due to the lack of a health sector regulator, the prices of medicinal products and medical devices are beginning to be regulated and other malpractices are being checked.

The government has set ambitious targets for disinvestment in order to improve the performance of public sector companies. It encourages companies / undertakings in the public sector to reorient themselves to remain relevant in the changing economic context. For example, the Post Office is all set to use its 1.5 lakh post offices to provide India Post Payments Bank services.

Under the motto of "minimum government, maximum governance," the government is increasing the use of digital technology to enable citizens to take advantage of basic public services, as well as creating a favorable environment for businesses and entrepreneurs.

Another rationale

In addition, a new rationale for government intervention stems from behavioral economics that justifies the government's role in influencing the behavior and choices of people. In fact, the government of Narendra Modi seeks to influence the thinking processes, behaviors and choices of people through social campaigns, such as promoting girls' children and making villages free of defecation.

The Prime Minister did not shy away from lending his own voice to urge people to practice yoga to stay healthy, to use khadi clothing that can help to generate income for khadi workers, to give up LPG subsidies for those who cannot afford it, to switch to LED bulbs for electricity conservation, and so on.

The above examples are only illustrative. Actually, the list of reforms / programs is much longer. The government has largely remained away from being populist in almost all its reforms / programs. Populism has not been chased by neglect of development. What he has successfully done is turn development into good politics. In this way, the overlap between development and politics could be maximized.

In a country with a huge development deficit compared to its people's rising aspirations, the government's attention lies in several areas. On many fronts, the government is moving at the same time. Directionally, it's okay, but how about the pace of reforms and the implementation of various programmes?

Narendra Modi — A True Patriot

When Modi took power in 2014 by winning the Lok Sabha election with a massive mandate, he sent a strong message: "We're not here for any positions, but for a responsibility." Everyone began to fall in line, from bureaucrats to mps. Whether it's strengthening foreign policy or launching welfare programs for the low-income group, the Modi team has worked hard to meet the expectations of people.

The Indian government led by Modi is clocking over four years at the wheel. Here are ten important things that the government of Modi has achieved since it took office:

Make in India

Narendra Modi launched a major national program to facilitate investment, boost research and development (R&D), ensure product originality and create skills-based jobs by setting up the industrial sector. With his idea of 'Make in India,' Modi has reached the world and generated positive response from foreign companies. The pipeline's key reform of the Labor Law will boost manufacturing and foreign investment in India.

Swachh Bharat Abhiyan (Clean India Campaign)

Modi launched Swachh Bharat Abhiyan on 2 Oct 2014. Filth is considered one of India's biggest problems and Modi has given due importance to the issue by launching a national campaign. Many called it Modi's masterstrike, as it placed him on par with Mahatma Gandhi in public perception and gave people the message to act on hygiene and civic sense. To promote the initiative, Modi has nominated significant personalities from the film industry, sports, media, business and other celebrities.

Creation of NITI Aayog to Replace Planning Commission

On 1 Jan 2015, Modi formed the National Institution for the Transformation of India (NITI) Aayog, an Indian government policy think-tank that replaced the Planning Commission. The panel was abolished together with goms and egoms that caused UPA policy paralysis. NITI Aayog is headed by PM Modi and its members include top economists, consultants and US think tank advisors.

Jan Dhan Yojana

On 15 August 2014, Jan Dhan Yojana was announced by Modi. Last year, more than 15 crore bank accounts were opened. The main focus was to reach every household in order to provide account holders with credit facilities, pensions and insurance.

Economic Reforms and Policy Implementation

The primary focus of the Modi-led NDA government is to revive the Indian economy through major manufacturing and export reforms. Not only has the government increased the limits of FDI in railways, insurance and defence, but it has also encouraged the privatization of public sector companies that cause losses. Modi continued to focus on transformation without being bogged down by coalition partners. On the infrastructure front, government work on connecting major metros under the Diamond Quadrilateral Rail Corridor project has already begun. For Modi's dream projects, major reforms and developments are underway: 100 Smart Cities and the Clean Ganga Mission.

Foreign Policy Put on Fast-track Mode

Modi's foreign policy is currently focussed on improving relations with neighbouring countries and getting the world to invest in India. He met several American business leaders in the United States and invited them to participate in the Make in India programme. He urged Airbus, the aerospace giant, to explore production opportunities in India during his recent visit to France. He made a strong pitch in Germany for the initiative Make in

India. He tried to send a message from India that was more "competitive, confident and secure." India.

Tourism Gets a Push

Tourism was prominently featured in the action plan of the government. Its main objective was to make India a world-class destination for travel. The visa system underwent a major renovation in the last year. A key step in this direction was the introduction of visa-on-arrival service for all leading nations. In addition, the number of foreign tourist arrivals after the Modi government came to power has reportedly seen growth.

Implementation of Neighbourhood First Policy

One of the Modi government's major policy initiatives was to actively focus on improving relations with immediate neighbours. Modi's aggressive and intelligent move as Prime Minister was to invite all the leaders of the SAARC nations to Modi's swearing-in ceremony. It gave the world a bold message that no one in Asia swears as we do. It was Modi's first diplomatic victory and India began to take itself seriously.

Campaign for Building Toilets

PM Modi has launched a huge project to build 10 crore toilets at an incredible rate of one toilet per second by 2019. In this Clean India drive, Modi appealed to the corporate sector for contribution. The positive response came from IT giant TCS and they decided to build 10,000 toilets in the country's girls ' schools. For this cause, a huge 100 crore fund has been provided. The Oriental Bank of Commerce has announced two crore's contribution to building toilets. The Bharti Foundation, Adani Group, Reliance Group and Vedanta Group also promised support for the campaign and made a significant contribution.

Confidence-building Measures in Kashmir

Kashmir is an integral part of India, but it has a long list of complaints from previous governments-both central and state. When the flood ravaged the valley, the Modi government's response was immediate and genuine. Constant monitoring system for areas and people in Kashmir affected by the flood. He also chose to spend Deepawali with survivors of the Kashmir flood. His critics even praised his move. An Indian politician managed to establish a connection with the Kashmiri people after a long time.

CHAPTER SEVEN

India through the scope

Laying the Foundation for Transformation

India is a country of contrasts today. It is one of the world's fastest-growing economies, but it is also a country with an immense, unfinished global development agenda. Poverty has fallen dramatically, but it has not benefited everyone equally. Sixty percent of India's poor live in seven low-income states, and poverty remains stubbornly high among the tribal population. There has been significant progress in education, health and maternal mortality, but some states face human development challenges similar to those in the world's poorest countries. Much remains to be done in India in order to succeed in global efforts to reduce poverty and improve human development.

Challenge

Although India's development has been one of the most remarkable global achievements in recent times, its gross national income ($ 1,570 per capita (2014, current US$)) remains low and significantly lags behind the comparative countries (Brazil, Russia, India, China, South Africa). Its challenges to development remain profound and complex. India is still home to nearly a quarter (270 million) of the world's poor, despite halving extreme poverty. Income inequality is on the rise, and structural inequalities have prevented whole groups (lower castes, tribes and women) from taking full advantage of the opportunities that recent economic growth has provided. India's participation in women's workforce is low and decreasing; only 27 percent of women aged 15 and over work. Maternal and child mortality rates remain stubbornly high and 38.7% of Indian children suffer from malnutrition. One of the country's greatest challenges has been to end open defecation in India's villages. An estimated 567 million people are still defecating in the open in India. The lack of access to sanitation has had a significant negative impact on the health and nutrition of children and women's safety. The country is rapidly urbanizing, with 10 million people migrating to towns and cities each year, leading to demands for better services, jobs, infrastructure, affordable housing and sound environmental management. India's overall needs for infrastructure remain massive. Some 250 million people do not have access to electricity and those who have to deal with unreliable supplies and frequent outages. One quarter of the rural population does not have access to all weather roads. Addressing these challenges is central not only to India and its people, but also to global progress on the new Sustainable Development Goals and efforts to reduce poverty and increase shared prosperity.

Solution

The Country Partnership Strategy of the World Bank Group (WBG) (FY2013-2017) supports the government's objective of faster, sustainable and inclusive growth. It seeks to address India's most pressing development challenges, especially in its poorest states -Bihar, Chhattisgarh, Jharkhand, Madhya Pradesh, Odisha, Rajasthan and Uttar Pradesh -where the fight against poverty must be won in order to make a significant contribution to the global rate of poverty by 2030. The WBG addresses these challenges with an integrated support package, which includes financing, advisory services, analytical work and capacity building in three broad areas:

Economic Integration: Improved domestic, regional and global integration will boost growth in India, as well as more balanced growth in its low-income and advanced countries. In order to promote economic integration, WBG support focuses on improving infrastructure -mainly transport and power; strengthening the manufacturing sector; developing a skilled workforce that can meet the needs of a rapidly growing economy; and improving the business environment in order to attract more private sector investment. The work continues to support several high-profile initiatives by the government, such as those aimed at providing power for all 24/7-with a particular focus on solar power, improving the business climate and helping to modernize India's massive railway system.

Rural-Urban Transformation: The faster a country urbanizes, the faster it grows, and the rapid growth of Indian cities. The number of towns increased from 5,000 (2001) to 8,000 (2011) in just one decade, and some 53 towns have over one million inhabitants. The WBG helps India tackle the many challenges of this massive rural to urban transformation by focusing on improving the "livability" of cities-providing better infrastructure, greater access to basic services and strengthening urban governments ' institutional capacity. Support for key initiatives includes the development of 100 intelligent cities across India and improved access to public services in more than 500 cities under the AMRUT programme. Without an equally strong focus on rural development, successful urbanization cannot take place. Therefore, India's efforts to manage its ongoing transformation are also central to improving the "livability" of India's villages, increasing agricultural productivity while creating more off-farm jobs. Recognizing that urbanization and sustained high economic growth can be both damaging to the environment and promoting energy efficiency and reducing greenhouse gas emissions, the WBG supports government efforts to better manage the environment in order to protect India's vast natural resources. In this area, the cleaning and rejuvenation of the iconic Ganga River, whose basin has a population of 450 million, is central to the Bank's support.

Inclusion: If India wants to realize its potential for sustained growth, poverty reduction and shared prosperity, it is essential to increase economic opportunities for all -irrespective of social grouping, age, gender or where they live. This will require significant improvements in the quality of education at all levels, improving health, nutrition and social protection, and creating more and better jobs. It will also call for greater attention to reduce gender inequities and create more opportunities for girls and women throughout India. One area of special concern is the decreasing rate of participation of women in the labor force, which is lower in urban areas than in rural areas. Through operations and analytical work, the World Bank Group focuses on addressing gender throughout a life cycle -from the womb to the classroom and the workplace. Since building skills will be crucial in order to ensure India's global competitiveness and inclusive growth, the World Bank is increasing its support for India's ambitious initiative "Skilling India," which aims to equip 500 million young people with skills for a changing labor market. Analytical skills work is increasingly taking a lifecycle approach, looking at a worker's lifetime and technical skills, from birth to education, training and beyond, and identifying the challenges at each stage. Since nutrition is the starting point, the Bank is intensifying efforts, together with domestic and international partners, to help India address its very high rate of child malnutrition.

Results

Support for India's development agenda by the International Development Association (IDA) has helped to improve health, education, rural development and increasingly manage disaster risks. Some results are shown below:

Education: Between 2001 and 2009, the Education for All Program in India enrolled some 20 million children outside school, in particular girls and children from socially disadvantaged families. By 2009, the number of children out of school had dropped to approximately 8.1 million. More than 98 percent of children in India now have access to a primary school within 1 kilometer of their home. The focus now is on improving the quality of education, keeping children in school and ensuring that more children have access to secondary education and complete it.

Support from the IDA for vocational training programs in selected institutions has helped more graduates find jobs, rising from just 32 percent in 2006 to more than 60 percent in 2011. Rural livelihood projects have trained 350,000 young people in the last three years, and 250,000 of them have been placed in jobs. The empowerment of large numbers of India's young people, especially in rural areas, with skills that are better suited to labor market demands-whether informal or formal-will help them find jobs in growing towns and cities where better-paid jobs are more readily available.

Rural livelihoods: In 90,000 villages, rural livelihood programs mobilized more than 30 million poor households into 1.2 million self-help groups (shgs)-up from 8 million in 2009. Of the SHG participants, 95 percent are women. In Andhra Pradesh alone, 10 million SHG women saw a 115 percent increase in their incomes. The savings of members exceeded $1.1 billion (2011) and access to credit increased by 200 percent to $5.8 billion (2000 -09). Local value-added activities carried out by these groups and their direct market links resulted in 30-40 percent higher prices for SHG products, which reduced trade conditions in favor of the poor in India.

Rural water supply and sanitation: IDA projects have contributed more than $1.4 billion in funding for rural water supply and sanitation over the past two decades. These programs have benefited approximately 24 million people in more than 15,000 villages, with populations ranging from 150 to 15,000. In addition, improved sanitation has benefited some 17 million rural people. Many projects have helped to promote the participation of women in meaningful discussions about changing old sanitation behaviors and decision-making on the use and maintenance of water and sanitation infrastructure.

Health: India has the world's greatest burden of tuberculosis (TB). An estimated 2.2 million new cases of tuberculosis occur each year in India, accounting for a quarter of the global burden. Between 1998 and 2012, two IDA credits totalling $279 million provided significant support for effective diagnosis and treatment in the context of the national program to control tuberculosis. During this period, the program diagnosed and treated more than 15 million people with TB, saving an estimated 2.6 million lives. To date, approximately 81 percent of women sex workers (FSW), 66 percent of men who have sex with men (MSM) and 71 percent of injecting drug users (IDU) have reached the national AIDS program supported by IDA, with targeted interventions. However, to secure these gains, continued attention is needed.

Support from the IDA for health projects has helped pregnant women to reach medical facilities in time for delivery; in Tamil Nadu, 99.5% of deliveries are now carried out in medical institutions. Despite rising rates of decline, however, maternal and child mortality rates in much poorer countries remain on an equal footing. And while India has recorded impressive economic growth in the last decade and the rate of malnutrition has declined, stunting rates remain significantly higher than in comparative countries such as the BRICS countries (Brazil, Russia, India, China, and South Africa).

Disaster management: Support for the National Cyclone Risk Mitigation Project (Phase I) financed and handed over to communities the construction of 420 cyclone shelters in Andhra Pradesh and the low-income state of Odisha. Due to the capacity of each shelter to accommodate 2,000 people, half a million people can now be kept safe during cyclones and other adverse weather conditions. In addition, these states have completed a total of 740 kilometers of roads, along with seven salt embankments and 20 bridges in the state of Andhra Pradesh.

Rural Roads: Since September 2004, some US$2 billion in support from the IDA has helped India's National Rural Roads Program to improve connectivity, particularly in economically weaker regions and hill states. Rural people in the states of Himachal Pradesh, Jharkhand, Meghalaya, Punjab, Rajasthan, Uttarakhand and Uttar Pradesh have benefited about 24,200 km of all-weather roads. Much more needs to be done, however, as one third of the rural population still lacks access to a weather-related road.

Agriculture and watershed development: Over the past decade or so, IDA support has helped farmers in Karnataka, Himachal Pradesh and Uttarakhand's rain-fed regions to implement measures to conserve soil and water and increase agricultural productivity. The lessons learned helped shape the Common Watershed Guidelines of the Indian Government and the design of national watershed programmes.

Since 1993, two projects to restore Sodic Lands in Uttar Pradesh have cultivated more than 260,000 hectares of barren or unproductive land. More than 425,000 poor families have benefited from an increase in crop yields three to six times. About 15,000 shgs helped women pool savings and connect to the formal network of banking. These shgs now manage the mid-day meal provided by a government program in local state schools in several villages. A $197 million credit from the World Bank is now supporting the third phase of the project aimed at reclaiming another 130,000 hectares of predominantly barren and low-productivity sodic lands in about 25 state districts.

Bank Group Contribution

The WBG supported India's efforts to address fundamental development challenges and build a modern economy as a long-term development partner. It has provided financing, knowledge, advisory services and technical assistance where and when it was most needed since the first IBRD loan to the Indian Railways in 1949. IDA has helped improve health, education and rural development outcomes. IDA supported India's efforts to tackle polio (polio has not occurred since January 2011), tuberculosis, leprosy, river blindness and HIV / AIDS, improving the lives of millions of people and contributing enormously to global efforts to control these diseases. WBG financing (especially IDA credits) and technical assistance played a key role in the Green Revolution-a landmark in India's development, which freed the country from dependence on food imports, turning it into a net exporter of food and helping millions to escape hunger and poverty. In education, IDA and the Department for International Development of the European Union and the United Kingdom played an important role in the universalization of primary education. As of 7 April 2015, the WB portfolio in India included 58 projects financed by the IDA (seven of which were mixed IBRD / IDA projects), totalling a net commitment of $12 billion. Approximately $2.6 billion for education, $2.5 billion for agriculture and rural development, $1.8 billion for disaster risk management, $1.3 billion for rural water and sanitation, and $613 million for health and nutrition. In supporting India's low-income countries to address their development challenges, the IDA continues to play an important role. More than half of all IDA commitments ($ 5.6 billion) in fiscal 2013-15 supported projects in these poor and isolated states.

Partners

By working closer with partners, IDA has leveraged its resources. For example, for more than a decade, it has been partnering in the education sector with the United Kingdom Department for International Development (DFID) and the European Commission, first in primary education and, more recently, in improving access, equity and quality at secondary level. IDA also co-finances three health operations throughout the country with DFID. Development cooperation

Market size

It is estimated that India's GDP increased by 6.6% in 2017-18 and is expected to grow by 7.3% in 2018-19. GDP (at constant 2011-12 prices) increased by 7.6 per cent in the first half of 2018-19. India has maintained its position as the world's third largest start-up base with more than 4,750 technology start-ups, with approximately 1,400 new start-ups established in 2016, according to a NASSCOM report. According to a study by the ASSOCHAM and Thought Arbitrage Research Institute, India's labor force is expected to reach 160-170 million by 2020, based on population growth rate, increased labor force participation and higher education enrolment, among other factors. India's foreign exchange reserves amounted to US$ 393.29 billion in the week until 21 December 2018, according to RBI data.

Recent Developments

With the economic scenario improving, various investments have been made in different sectors of the economy. M&A activity in India increased by 53.3 percent to 77.6 billion dollars in 2017, while private equity deals reached 24.4 billion dollars. Some of the recent important developments in the Indian economy are as follows: In

April-November 2018, India's exports increased by 15.48 percent year-on-year to US$ 351.99 billion. In December 2018, the Nikkei India Manufacturing Purchasing Managers' Index (PMI) stood at 53.2. Activity in the country in mergers and acquisitions (M&A) reached $82.1 billion in 2018 (until November). Income tax collection in the country between April and November 2018 reached Rs 2.50 lakh crore (US$ 35.88 billion). Companies in India raised about US$5.52 billion in 2018 (until November) through initial public offerings (IPO). India's inflow of foreign direct investment (FDI) amounted to US$389.60 billion between April 2000 and June 2018, with the highest contribution from services, computer software and hardware, telecommunications, construction, trade and automobiles. In April-October 2018, India's Industrial Production Index (IIP) increased by 5.6 percent year-on-year. Inflation in the consumer price index (CPI) increased from 3.38% in October 2018 to 2.33% in November 2018. In 2017, approximately 10.8 million jobs were created in India. India improved its ranking in the Doing Business Report of the World Bank by 23 spots over its ranking in 2017 and ranked 77 among 190 countries in the report's 2019 edition. According to T V Mohan Das Pai, Chairman of Manipal Global Education, India is expected to have 100,000 startups by 2025, which will create jobs for 3.25 million people and a value of US$ 500 billion. The World Bank has stated that private investments in India are expected to increase by 8.8 per cent in the 2018-19 financial year to exceed 7.4 per cent growth in private consumption, thereby driving growth in India's gross domestic product (GDP) in the 2018-19 financial year. India, according to the World Bank's Migration and Development Brief, is expected to retain its position as the world's leading recipient of remittances in 2018, with total remittances reaching US$ 80 billion.

Government Initiatives

Mr Arun Jaitley, Minister of Finance of the Union, Government of India, announced the Union budget for 2018-19 in Parliament on 1 February 2018. The year's budget focused on boosting the rural economy and strengthening the agricultural sector, providing health care for the economically disadvantaged, creating infrastructure and improving the country's education quality. According to the budget, the government is committed to doubling the income of farmers by 2022. A total of Rs 14.34 lakh crore (USD 196.94 billion) will be spent in rural areas to create livelihoods and infrastructure. Infrastructure budget allocations for 2018-19 are set at Rs 5.97 lakh crore (USD 81.99 billion). There have always been high allocations for the rail and road sectors. According to the International Labor Organization (ILO), India's unemployment rate is expected to be 3.5% in 2018. Due to various government initiatives such as Make in India and Digital India, many foreign companies are setting up their facilities in India. India's Prime Minister, Mr. Narendra Modi, launched the Make in India initiative with the aim of boosting the Indian economy's manufacturing sector, increasing the purchasing power of an average Indian consumer, which, in addition to benefiting investors, would further boost demand and thus stimulate development. Under the Make in India initiative, India's government is seeking to boost the manufacturing sector's contribution and aims to take up to 25 percent of GDP from the current 17 percent. In addition, the government has also developed an initiative on Digital India, which focuses on three key components: Digital infrastructure creation, digital service delivery and digital literacy.

Some of the government's recent initiatives and developments are discussed below: The National Institute for the Transformation of India (NITI) Aayog published a strategic document entitled "Strategy for New India @75" to help India become an economy of US$ 4 trillion by the year 23. India's government will increase public health spending by 2025 to 2.5% of GDP. India's government released the 2018 maiden agricultural export policy, which aims to double the country's agricultural exports by 2022 to US$ 60 billion. Under the Indian government's housing scheme Pradhan Mantri Awas Yojana (Urban), approximately 1.29 million houses were built until 24

December 2018. In April 2018, electrification of villages in India was completed. Under Pradhan Mantri Sahaj Bijli Har Ghar Yojana (SAUBHAGYA), approximately 22.43 million households were electrified until 17 December 2018. In addition, as of December 2018, 100 per cent of household electrification was already achieved in 25 states. According to the Cabinet Committee on Economic Affairs (CCEA), the Employment Generation Program of the Prime Minister (PMEGP) will continue with an expenditure of Rs 5,500 crore (US$ 755.36 million) for three years from 2017-18 to 2019-20.

The objective of an open defecation free (ODF) India will be achieved by 2 October 2019, as the Swachh Bharat Mission (Gramin) has adequate funding available, according to Ms Uma Bharti, Minister of Drinking Water and Sanitation, Government of India. India's government has decided to invest Rs 2.11 trillion (USD 32.9 billion) over the next two years to recapitalize public-sector banks and Rs 7 trillion (USD 109.31 billion) over the next five years to build new roads and roads. As of November 2018, Rs 82,000 crore (USD 11.75 billion) was already infused and by March 2019, the government plans to infuse Rs 42,000 crore (USD 6.02 billion). The Indian Ministry of Commerce and Industry, Government of India, released a mid-term review of India's Foreign Trade Policy (FTP) 2015-2020, according to which annual incentives for labor-intensive MSME sectors increased by 2 percent.

Road Ahead

India's gross domestic product (GDP) is expected to reach US$ 6 trillion by FY27 and achieve upper-middle-income status on the basis of digitization, globalization, favorable demographics and reforms. India's revenue receipts are estimated to reach Rs 28-30 trillion (USD 385-412 billion) by 2019, owing to Indian government measures to strengthen infrastructure and reforms such as demonization and the GST. India also focuses on renewable energy sources. By 2030, it plans to achieve 40% of its energy from non-fossil sources, which is currently 30%, and it also plans to increase its renewable energy capacity by 2022 from 175 GW. India is expected to be the third largest consumer economy, since its consumption may triple to US$ 4 trillion by 2025, due to changes in consumer behavior and expenditure, according to a report from the Boston Consulting Group (BCG), and it is estimated that the United States will be the second largest economy in terms of purchasing power parity (PPP) by 2040, according to a report from the pricewaterhouse.

CHAPTER EIGHT

India's path to Prosperity

India faced major economic challenges when Prime Minister Narendra Modi took office in May 2014. In the last two years of the outgoing government, growth fell to 5.9 percent, down from a nine-year average of 8.2 percent. Inflation averaged 9.7 percent over the same two years. In the meantime, the government was in a state of paralysis, unable to control corruption or complete large-scale projects and needed key structural reforms. The Modi government has largely managed to address these problems four years later. On average, inflation has come down to 4.3 percent and growth has climbed to 7.3 percent over the last four years. Bold steps such as the November 2016 demonetization program have helped curb corruption. And the government has introduced numerous initiatives to improve efficiency, such as the replacement of a complex set of central and state taxes with a single tax on goods and services (GST). These policies put India together on the road to long-term growth and prosperity.

Boosting efficiency

Improving governance and efficiency has been one of Modi's main focal points since taking office. Deep paralysis has characterized the last two years of the outgoing government under Prime Minister Manmohan Singh. Large projects were stalled due to a lack of coordination between various ministries and excessive environmental clearance delays. When Modi took office, he intervened directly to accelerate clearances and decision-making. He established a process by which he himself regularly chairs meetings of senior ministry staff relevant to decision-making on specific projects and policy issues.

Early in its tenure, the government also made significant efforts at state level to simplify and digitize different clearances for companies. This effort led to an unprecedented jump from 140 to 100 between 2014 and 2018 in India's position in the World Bank Ease of Doing Business rankings. At the same time, the government has also taken steps to simplify the lives of citizens. In the past, job and school applicants had to go through a difficult process in which senior officials or judges certified diploma copies. This decades-long practice has been replaced by a self-certification policy that relieves everyone, especially rural residents. Citizens can also store digital copies of their diplomas using the state's free service, and many government services are now available online. The government also provided 40 million poor rural households with stoves that use liquid petroleum gas instead of black carbon from wood-burning stoves and coal-burning stoves.

India also took up the fight against corruption under Modi. His most audacious measure on this front was demonetization, which ended on 8 November 2016 with a legal tender status of 500 and 1,000 rupee notes. The move temporarily wiped out 86 percent of the circulating national currency. Holders of these notes had to deposit them in bank accounts in order to eventually receive new currency bills. The government had hoped that for fear of being caught, those holding unaccounted wealth in these notes would not deposit them. This was not the case, as most holders found ways to work around the program. Many of them sold the notes to those who could play the system for more wealth than they actually held. Subsequent analyzes of bank accounts have, however, led to the detection and closure of hundreds of thousands of fake shell companies and the disqualification of a similarly large number of company directors in the future. The demonetization also led to a 25 percent decrease in real estate value, which eroded a significant amount of black wealth in buildings and structures. Finally, demonetization has sent a strong signal of the government's determination to combat corruption, which has led to an increase in the number of payers of income taxes and the notification of illegal transactions.

By replacing the former Planning Commission with the National Institution for the Transformation of India (NITI), Modi also significantly improved government efficiency. A bipartisan consensus has evolved over time that the Planning Commission has lost its relevance with India moving towards a market economy since the reforms of 1991. However, no previous government has done anything to replace it with a more contemporary institution that is market-friendly. The NITI was launched in 2015 as an active promoter of the Prime Minister's reform agenda. It has also established a fairer relationship between the center and the states. It offers policy advice to states on the one hand, while seeking advice in the formulation of central government policies on the other.

Special projects

Until now, the former's ability to complete projects on scale and at speed has been a significant difference between China and India. India finally saw at least some progress in this direction under Modi. There are three specific examples worth mentioning: The spread of biometric identity cards, the opening of bank accounts for Jan Dhan and the construction of toilets under the Swacch Bharat Mission (SBM).

Firstly, all residents of the country are issued a biometric identity card. The Aadhaar project, which was started under the previous government in 2010, has now distributed 1,2 billion such cards, and almost all Indian residents, except those in a few border states, have one. In August 2017 alone, the government issued 8.65 million cards. As part of its efforts to increase financial inclusion, the government launched the Jan Dhan bank account program and in August 2014 opened 18 million bank accounts for citizens in just one week, which qualified for inclusion in the Guinness Book of World Records. The total number of bank accounts of Jan Dhan now stands at 316 million.

Finally, the proportion of rural households with toilets rose from barely 38 percent to 84.2 percent under SBM. When Modi took office, the number of states without open defecation increased from none to 17. Modi is now within reach of his declared goal: An open-defecation-free India by the 150th birthday of Mahatma Gandhi on October 2, 2019.

Structural reforms

When Modi came to office, structural reform momentum was lost and little progress was made in the last five years. Significant progress has been made in many areas during his tenure. Although the full list is too long to be fully covered, some key reforms are worth noting: The deregulation of gasoline and diesel prices, further opening up to foreign direct investment (FDI), greater flexibility in the labor market, the shift to direct transfers of benefits (DBT), the tax on goods and services (GST), and the Insolvency and Bankruptcy Code (IBC).

India has deregulated the price of petrol and diesel under Modi. For too long, state subsidies reduced prices paid by consumers, thus promoting wasteful consumption of products and adding to the fiscal deficit. These subsidies have now been completely removed. During the recent rise in crude prices, which led to significant increases in retail gasoline and diesel prices, voices were raised from almost all quarters to lower prices, but the government did not restore subsidies. The subsidy for liquid petroleum gas used in cooking has also been significantly reduced in the last four years.

Modi has also opened up more foreign direct investment (FDI) in India. When he came to office, foreign investors saw a relaxation of the FDI cap in the insurance market from 26% to 49% as a litmus test of his determination to put India back on the path of reform. Not only did the Modi government deliver on this reform, but it went further by opening up FDI defense. It also allowed 100% FDI in the marketing of food products produced in India, high-tech and capital-intensive railway activities, medical device manufacturing and the e-commerce market. The last of these items led to Amazon and Walmart entering the e-commerce space in India. The total flow of FDI, which averaged $35 billion in the outgoing government's last two fiscal years, increased to $60 billion in the fiscal year ending in March 2017 and $48 billion in the nine-month period from April to December 2017.

Under one of the labor laws, a manufacturing company with 100 or more employees cannot terminate employees for any reason without the permission of the relevant regulatory authority, which is practically never granted. Companies in India have therefore tended to remain small, particularly in labor-intensive sectors with small margins per worker. In order to alleviate this problem, the government has now introduced fixed-term employment in all sectors, enabling companies to hire workers for a specified term, after which they will not be able to remain. This will make hiring companies more flexible than in the past.

In order to improve the efficiency of the distribution of benefits under social programs and to curb waste, fraud and abuse, the government has increasingly channeled its benefits through the Direct Benefit Transfer (DBT) mechanism, which requires beneficiaries to produce their Aadhaar biometric identity cards. The DBT mechanism is now implementing a vast number of benefits, including major benefits such as subsidies for cooking gas cylinders, the sale of food grain at subsidized prices, and the payment of salaries for employment under the National Rural Employment Guarantee Act. This has allowed tens of millions of fantasy beneficiaries to be eliminated. Cumulative savings from the DBT mechanism exceed $10 billion.

The GST, meanwhile, was over a decade a reform in the making. The government has finally completed this complex reform successfully, requiring consensus across 29 states, a constitutional amendment and multiple laws. Although the reform has been criticized for maintaining up to four different tax rates and poor implementation, its main benefit is the replacement of numerous indirect taxes at central and state level by a single tax on each product at national level. A major logistics company, Rivigo, already reports that, with the GST leading to the removal of checkpoints at state borders, travel time for trucks on roads has decreased by 15 percent on average.

The GST, meanwhile, was over a decade a reform in the making. The government has finally completed this complex reform successfully, requiring consensus across 29 states, a constitutional amendment and multiple laws. Although the reform has been criticized for maintaining up to four different tax rates and poor implementation, its main benefit is the replacement of numerous indirect taxes at central and state level by a single tax on each product at national level. A major logistics company, Rivigo, already reports that, with the GST leading to the removal of checkpoints at state borders, travel time for trucks on roads has decreased by 15 percent on average.

The future of the Indian economy

There is one important area in which it has fallen short of all the economic achievements of the Modi government: international trade. The top industrial tariff (with some exceptions, such as textiles, clothing and cars) was reduced from 355 percent to 10 percent by 2007 by a concerted reduction in trade barriers beginning in 1991. Correspondingly, the average industrial rate fell from 113 percent to 12 percent. But the government has recently returned to the discredited policy of industrialization of import-substitution, which promotes industrialization by replacing imports with domestic production and raising tariffs on a large number of products.

At present, about 45% of India's workforce remains in agriculture, which produces only 15% of GDP. Economic change requires the creation of well-paid jobs in industry and services, so that a significant proportion of the current agricultural workforce can migrate from their current low-productivity jobs. If this migration is to take place quickly, India must significantly increase its share of global exports, in particular labor-intensive products. With China withdrawing from these products because of its high salaries, this is a feasible proposal, but only if India's own policies favor an external orientation towards the policy of import substitution.

The Modi government has made great progress in reforming the economy over the past four years in order to achieve greater growth and prosperity. Although many of its policies have already had a significant effect, most will only have their full impact in the longer term, so the prospects for further growth and prosperity are excellent unless the next government becomes populist.

India: The road to wider prosperity

Let's discuss what should be next election resolution for India. Prime Minister Narendra Modi, while addressing a joint meeting of the US Congress on June 8, 2016, shared his dream: "empowering every Indian through many social and economic transformations".

India must address a variety of contemporary issues for this. The most important issue for sustainable and inclusive India is human development. In recent years, the development economy has become more people-centered than before. It has rediscovered that people are both the means and the end of the process of economic development and that this process becomes hollow rhetoric without human development. India must therefore quickly develop an agenda to speed up human development. And this will help solve most of today's India's problems, as I strongly believe in the phrase: Change One Thing and All Changes.

The concept of skills is central to human development. Almost everyone's basic skills include: Good health, access to knowledge and decent living standards. Other capabilities central to a fulfilling life may include the ability to participate in decisions that affect one's life and control one's living environment. HD is therefore about real freedom that ordinary people must decide who they should be, what they should do and how they should live. In many developing countries, HD-based strategies have been used as a weapon to empower people; they have proven quite effective.

Why the development of human beings? The UNDP Human Development Report 2016 does not highlight India's achievement in expanding the capacity of people and improving their well-being. In the Human Development Index, India ranks 131 out of 188. This puts it in the category of' medium.' The HDI combines the average health, education and income achievements of a country. Bill Gates and Ratan Tata commented on India's HDI listing: "Human capital is one of India's biggest assets. Yet the fastest-growing economy in the world has not touched the bottom of the economic pyramid on millions of Indian citizens."

India houses for the few comfort enclaves, but for the many they are by no means redemptive. According to Lucas Chancel, co-director of the World Inequality Lab at the Paris School of Economics, inequality has actually accelerated in recent decades. In the early 1980s, India's top 1 percent richest individuals captured 6 percent of total income, and the value is now 22 percent. Overall,

India's lowest 50 percent (approximately 650 million people or 130 million families) still has little access to basic goods such as quality education, health or health care. In terms of investments for the lowest income groups, therefore, much more can be done. "this will significantly increase the rate of income growth at the bottom and the economic growth rate as a whole."

This strongly supports the need for India to turn its vast deprived population into a competitive advantage by increasing productivity, and human development is one of the most important (or only) stimulants to achieve this result.

HD's definition of "expanding the choices of people" is very broad, covering many problems. One has to shorten it. First, human development must focus on improving the quality of education; improving primary health; strengthening WASH factors (water, sanitation and hygiene), reducing gender gaps; and most importantly, stabilizing the population by reducing the incidence of undesirable childbearing and infant mortality. We also recognize that the shift of access labor from agriculture to non-agricultural sectors and the management of climate change, including air quality, are also important inputs in the human development process.

The five areas we focus on in this section do not provide a comprehensive agenda for unlocking human potential, but these are believed to be among the most important inputs in the prevailing situation if pursued as a package, as noted below:

Ensuring quality school education:

Is India's education system sufficiently geared to meet the low-productivity challenge? One cannot be too optimistic about India's poor education system from top to bottom. Elementary education is the first step towards improving the quality of education. India's school education is facing many problems, but the following four areas are crucial:

1) Empowering teacher,

2) Strengthening vocational education,

3) Promoting digital technology, and

4) Enhancing community participation.

Promoting healthy life:

Ultimately, positive health outcomes contribute to better educational outcomes and a more productive and skilled workforce. India must therefore make its young population a competitive advantage, and primary health and nutrition are the basis for this outcome that promotes healthy living.

Most of India's health system's challenges can be attributed to investment and inefficient use of resources. A lack of doctors, inadequate training and a poor network of public hospitals, combined with bureaucratic bungling, mean that India often struggles to spend even its meager budgets. As a result, if health is not prioritized, the promise of universal health coverage will remain unfulfilled.

An effective healthcare system that addresses both communicable and non-communicable healthcare needs is urgently needed. India must therefore adopt an integrated national health care system based on a strong public primary care system with a clearly articulated supporting role for the private and indigenous sectors in the secondary and tertiary sectors.

Improving WASH factors:

UNDP emphasizes that clean water and adequate sanitation can lead to human development or break it. Data from the World Health Organization and UNICEF, among others, show that the poorest, young and women and girls suffer the most from poor WASH services. Therefore, improvements to WASH represent good economic investment in order to unlock human potential, since better WASH facilities mean good health and higher levels of school performance, which means higher productivity. "a World Bank study estimates that almost 40% of India's children are physically and cognitively stunted, mainly due to lack of sanitation. Such a large proportion of our future workforce cannot achieve their full production capacity poses a serious threat to the greatest strength -our demographic dividend,"

In other words, the social determinants of the human development agenda are better living conditions. Any improvement in access to toilet facilities, water, electricity and LPG is likely to lead to a significant reduction in domestic drudgery, especially for girls / women, which will free up their time for other activities, including schooling and professional life.

Promoting gender equality:

If the condition of women is not improved, it is impossible to think about India's welfare and sustainable development. It seems that we are frightened by the female abhivyakti (expression), khvaab (dream), or kalpana (fantasy). And by hook and crook, we want to regulate it. It seems that "women are not born, but made;" what better than India to illustrate this statement made about 70 years ago by Simone de Beauvoir. Therefore, the chains that bind women are not only external, but invisibly welded together by the dint of growing up in a patriarchal society that is still. We must therefore create a favorable environment in which women can pursue great dreams and contribute to the welfare and development of the country. Therefore, it is important to address the root causes of gender discrimination by son-preference and daughter-neglect. One must recognize that high GDP or economic growth alone does not automatically empower women or reduce inequality between women and men.

So what are we doing? Expanding education and employment opportunities will undoubtedly help achieve gender equality, but it may take longer. In order to speed up the process, "we need men to be allies," as Melinda Gates, co-chair of theBill and Melinda Gates Foundation, said in her article: Women Transform Societies, based on Indian experience. She expands her argument and writes: "The empowerment of women cannot just be about women; it must also be about men -fathers, brothers, husbands and sons -with whom they live their lives."

India's sex ratio is by population the worst among the world's ten largest countries-and it has worsened. Indian figures showed that there are 108 men per 100 women, compared to China's 106. The path ahead therefore looks long, winding and hazy. The present administration, however, shows the promise and will, albeit slowly, to clean the way. India is very fortunate that the present government recognizes that gender equality is part of the country's future; and campaigns such as "Beti Bachao, Beti Padhao (save the girl child, educate the girl child) will help to stop the epidemic of missing girls by eliminating gender inequality. In addition, there is a strong emphasis on changing mentality through training, awareness-raising, awareness-raising and mobilization on the ground.

Stabilizing population:

With India facing a host of major crises related to poverty, governance, corruption (especially on a daily basis), social and religious conflicts, why should anyone worry about the population? The simple answer is that virtually all the major problems facing India today are related to the galloping population in some critical way. With already high density and low living standards, a continued increase in the number means that the tragedy continues. The country already has more than 1,335 million people (2017) and each decade adds more than 160 million, with 12 million young people joining the workforce each year.

China and India are the world's two most populous countries. China's population was 302 million more than India in 1990. Due to India's higher population growth, the difference in population between these two countries is rapidly decreasing. China's population is 70 million more than India in 2017. And India will be the world's most populous country with around 1.45 billion people in 2025. This has increased the pressure on natural or administrative resources. India's population density is 450 people per square kilometer compared to China's 150 in 2017. India is three times thicker than China. The table also shows that population pressure has increased significantly since 1990, measured in terms of persons per square km. In the last 27 years it has increased slightly less than twice, while the corresponding figure for China is 1.2 times. China is the fourth largest country and India is the seventh largest country in area

The current growth in India's population is primarily driven by unwanted fertility. About three in ten pregnancies are unintended / unplanned or simply unwanted by the women who experience them, and these pregnancies lead to births that stimulate the continued growth of the population. Every year, approximately 27 million children are born in India and about 7-8 million births could be classified as unwanted. It is estimated that around 450 million of India's 1,335 million people in 2017 were the result of unwanted pregnancies, according to the National Family Health Surveys. How can one think of using them for the nation building with such a large number of people resulting from unwanted pregnancies? Despite concerted development efforts since 1991, the consequences of unwanted pregnancy are reflected in widespread malnutrition, poor health, poverty, analphabetism, unemployment, regressive governance and increasing scarcity of basic resources such as food, water and space.

How to implement the HD agenda?

The implementation strategy is based on a "whole child" concept for human development efforts-that is, the child and his / her family. Therefore, the book proposes a framework for unlocking human potential. All government school children aged 6-14 and their families will be at the center of attention. If necessary, all selected inputs for human development will be provided. Additional inputs may be added to meet the needs of specific people / area, so this framework is called "." In the 1990s and 2000s, government agencies will implement it in collaboration with civil organizations such as the pulsepolio campaign. In addition, the focus of different government programs such as Swachh Bharat, Skill India, Beti Bachao, Beti Padhao, Ujjwala Yojana, Saubhagya Yojana, etc. Will be on government-school-going children's families.

Today, the main concern is the impairment of human potential, which prevents India from reaping its rich demographic dividend. Therefore, human development is more than an objective in itself. It is a prerequisite for addressing the challenges of reducing inequality, promoting sustainable development and establishing good governance. It is high time India's government and research institutions focused on developing an effective and intelligent agenda for human development to unlock human potential.

CHAPTER NINE

Why India Needs a competent leaders in office

To properly discuss the above heading, it is important we take a broad look at what "Election" entails; with this, we can then decide if we are on the right track as well as our political leaders are on the track too;

Functions Of Elections

Elections play a key role in democratic governance. Because in most modern societies, direct democracy -a form of government in which political decisions are taken directly by the whole body of qualified citizens -is impractical, democratic government must be carried out through representatives. Elections enable voters to select leaders and to hold them accountable for their performance in office. Accountability can be undermined if the elected leaders do not care whether they are re-elected or if, for historical or other reasons, one party or coalition is so dominant that alternative candidates, parties or policies are effectively unable to choose.

However, the ability to control leaders by requiring them to participate in regular and regular elections helps to solve the problem of leadership succession and thus contributes to the continuation of democracy. In addition, where the electoral process is competitive and forces candidates or parties to expose their records and future intentions to popular scrutiny, elections serve as forums for public debate and public opinion expression. Elections therefore provide citizens with political education and ensure that democratic governments respond to the people's will. They also legitimize the acts of those who exercise power, a function that is even carried out to some extent by non-competitive elections.

Elections also strengthen the political community's stability and legitimacy. Elections, like national holidays commemorating common experiences, link citizens to each other and thus confirm the viability of politics. Elections therefore help facilitate social and political integration.

Finally, elections serve a purpose of self-realization by confirming the value and dignity of individual citizens as human beings. Whatever other voters need, participation in an election strengthens their self-esteem and self-respect. Voting gives people the chance to have their say and to satisfy their need to feel a sense of belonging by expressing partisanship. Even non-voting meets some people's need to express their alienation from the political community. For precisely these reasons, the long struggle for the right to vote and the demand for equal participation in elections can be seen as a manifestation of a deep human desire for personal fulfillment.

Elections are ritualistic, whether held under authoritarian or democratic regimes. Elections and then preceding campaigns are dramatic events accompanied by rallies, banners, posters, buttons, headlines and television coverage, all of which highlight the importance of participation in the event. The symbols of nationalism or patriotism, reform or revolution, past glory or future promise are invoked by candidates, political parties and interest groups representing various objectives. Whatever the peculiar national, regional or local variations, elections are events that break the monotony of everyday life and focus attention on the common fate by exciting emotions and channeling them to collective symbols.

Types of Elections

Elections of officeholders

Electoral authorities only have a limited power to determine government policies. Most elections do not directly establish public policy, but rather give a small group of officials the authority to make policies on behalf of the electorate as a whole (through laws and other devices).

Core to the election of officeholders are political parties. The selection and nomination of candidates, a vital first phase of the electoral process, is usually in the hands of political parties; an election is only the final process in the recruitment of political offices. The party system can therefore be considered an extension of the electoral process. Political parties provide the talent pool from which candidates are drawn, simplify and direct election choice and mobilize the electorate at the registration and election stage.

Political parties ' predominance over the electoral process has not gone unchallenged. For example, to limit the influence of political parties, some municipalities in the United States and Canada regularly hold non-partisan elections (in which party affiliations are not formally indicated on ballots). Non-partisanship in the United States began in the early 20th century as a reform movement and was partly intended to isolate local politics from state and national politics. In the last decades of the 20th century, the importance of political parties in many democratic countries declined as "candidate-centered" politics emerged and campaigning and accountability became highly personalized.

Recall elections

Like most populist innovations, it is an attempt to minimize the influence of political parties on representatives that recall office holders. The recall, which is widely adopted in the United States, is intended to ensure that an elected official acts in the interests of his constituency rather than his political party or his own conscience. The actual recall instrument is usually a letter of resignation signed before taking office by the elected representative. During the term of office, a quorum of constituents may evoke the letter if the performance of the representative does not meet its expectations.

The recall was successfully used against different types of officials in the United States, including judges, mayors and even state governors. Although the recall is not widely used in practice, it was used to remove governors in North Dakota (1921) and California (2003), even in jurisdictions where it is constitutionally provided for. After a bitter partisan struggle between Democrats and Republicans over workers ' rights to collective bargaining, Wisconsin experienced the single largest recall attempt in U.S. history in 2011; six Republicans and three Democrats faced a recall vote in the 33-member Senate, although only two senators-both Republicans-were defeated.

Referendum and initiative

The referendum and initiative are elections in which the preferences of the community on a particular issue are assessed; while the former are initiated by those in government, the latter are initiated by electoral groups.

Such devices, as forms of direct democracy, reflect a reluctance to entrust elected representatives with full decision-making power. Since voting participation in these types of elections is often quite low, however, voting in referendums and initiatives can be more easily influenced by political parties and interest groups than voting in elections for office holders.

Referendums are often used to raise and spend public money on bond issues, although they are occasionally used to decide on certain social or moral issues -such as restrictions on abortion or divorce -on which the elected bodies are not considered to have special competence. Referendums may be legally binding or merely consultative, but it is likely that even consultative referendums are considered legislative mandates. In Switzerland, which held approximately half of the world's national referendums, referendums and initiatives were used most heavily at national level. Evidence from Switzerland has shown that legislative referendums are more likely to succeed than public referendums. For example, approximately half of all laws and almost three-fourths of all constitutional changes initiated by the Swiss government were passed, while only about one-tenth of all citizens ' initiatives were successful. Switzerland, like the United States, also makes extensive use of referendums and initiatives at local and regional levels. At the end of the 20th century, referendums were more frequently used around the world than in previous years, especially in Europe, where referendums were held to decide public policy on voting systems, treaties and peace agreements (e.g. the Treaty on European Union) and social issues.

Plebiscite

Plebiscites are elections held to determine two key types of political issues: the legitimacy of the government and the nationality of territories challenged by governments. In the former case, the incumbent government uses a plebiscite to establish its right to speak for the nation, seeking a popular mandate as a basis for legitimacy. Plebiscites of this nature are thought to establish a direct relationship between the rulers and the ruled; intermediaries such as political parties are bypassed, which is why plebiscites are sometimes regarded as anti-pluralism and anti-competitive policies. The plebiscite was widely popular in France after the French Revolution in 1789, rooted in the ideas of nationalism and popular sovereignty. Totalitarian regimes used plebiscites to legitimize their rule in the 20th century.

Plebiscites have also been used as a tool for determining territorial nationality. For example, after the First World War, the League of Nations proposed 11 such plebiscites, the most successful of which was held in the Saar in 1935, until the end of the war, a state of Germany administered by the League for 15 years. However, this use of plebiscites is relatively rare, as it requires the prior agreement of the governments concerned on a usually highly contentious issue.

Systems Of Vote Counting

Individual votes are translated into collective decisions by a wide range of counting rules accepted by voters and leaders as legitimate prior to the election. In principle, these rules may require a plurality vote, which only requires the winner to have the highest number of votes; an absolute majority vote, which requires the winner to receive more than half the total number of votes; an extraordinary majority vote, which requires a higher proportion of the winner (e.g. a two-thirds majority); a proportional vote, which requires a political vote.

Legislative elections

There are a wide range of electoral systems for the allocation of legislative seats. Legislative electoral systems can in practice be classified into three broad categories: Plurality and majority systems (collectively referred to as majority systems), proportional systems and hybrid or semi-proportional systems. The electoral system is an important variable in explaining public policy decisions, since it determines the number of political parties that can be represented and thus participate in government.

The leadership of Modi

Four years ago, under Narendra Modi's leadership, the BJP was entrusted with the responsibility to increase the country's respect and to work for its overall development. This mandate was not just to change the prime minister or government, but to change the country. In the last three years, this has been visible. PM Modi touched 125 crore Indians ' minds. He has injected new hope and energy into a broken morality, dispersed systems and altered India's old mindsets. Modi has brought the common man closer to his social responsibilities through his addresses and campaigns. The fact that Modi talks in his speeches about the challenges of everyday life makes him the only hope for a solution to the problems of the common man.

Has any PM ever raised Clean India's issue from Red Fort ramparts? Living in filth almost became this country's destiny. It is true that achieving this goal will take some time, but at least people have begun to think about it. Did anyone imagine a PM campaigning to empower our daughters with programs like Beti Bachao, Beti Padhao? Has any PM launched a national campaign to preserve our country's rivers? Has any PM ever appealed to doctors one day a month to treat lactating mothers free of charge?

Has any PM ever urged students not to worry about examinations and focus instead on building a good character? Has any PM appealed to conserve water for old and young people? Has any PM ever made efforts to double farmers' income? Everyone knew the problems facing poor women in their kitchens, but did anyone make a more concrete effort than the Ujjwala plan? The Modi government has also made efforts to introduce free medical insurance, among other things, to check the rising prices of medicines.

Everyone was dissatisfied with the culture of the red beacon, but only Modi had the courage to scrap it in one swoop. Everyone knows about Pakistan's cowardly threats and cross-border terror, but no one thought it would give them an appropriate response by conducting surgical strikes. Many such examples show that PM Modi has his finger on the nation's pulse. As a result, he has become a reliable source of hope, strength and people's voice.

The trust of the common man in Modi is not without reason -it's because he's not sitting on a pedestal, but in their hearts. He connects with them when he says he's not the prime minister, but the people's "primary servant." He's not just talking, but he's implementing his energetic art.

The PM has a clear vision to ensure that every word becomes an inspiration for the country. Under BJP

President Amit Shah's leadership, lakhs of workers take every campaign to every corner of the country diligently. They work to become couriers of change to build a new India with the help of the media and social media.

Immediately after becoming PM, Modi made it clear at the BJP's parliamentary party meeting that his government will be dedicated to the poor and will work for villages, farmers, Dalits, the exploited, the victims, the deprived, young people and women. He fulfilled these promises.

PM Modi has introduced more than 105 programs for the country's development and the welfare of the poor in the last four years. Some of these, such as the schemes introduced for the poor, are important to mention-under these, the government will use funds obtained from deposits of black money to develop the poor. Another unique initiative was the scheme of Jan Dhan. At present, 1.26 lakh Bank Mitras are at work and 22.18 rupay debit cards have been issued to those on society's fringes who never thought they would enter a bank.

Similarly, more than 10 crore people have been registered under the Security Insurance Plan. This scheme has also benefited more than 10,000 people. Under the Pradhan Mantri Jeevan Jyoti Bima Yojana, more than 3 crore people have been enrolled and 61,000 people have already benefited. Under the National Health Policy, there is a provision in government hospitals for free checks and medicines for the poor. The poor are also covered by Rs 1 lakh medical insurance. Two poor crore families have been given free gas connections through the Ujjwala Yojana-by 2019, more than five poor core families will have free gas connections. There is no greater empowerment scheme for women.

The PM approved Rs 43,000 crore for the Deen Dayal Upadhyaya Gram Jyoti Yojana to fulfill its promise to provide 24/7 power. Work on ensuring that electricity reaches all homes by 2019 is underway. Every village will have electricity by May 1, 2018. This government works hard to ensure that by 2021 all poor people have their own homes. The poor will receive a lower interest rate for home loans. The crop insurance scheme will help farmers cope with natural disaster losses.

Each section of the country has been affected by the PM in the last four years. He talks to border soldiers and school students. Through his radio program, Mann ki Baat, he dealt with issues such as water conservation, changing perceptions of the disabled, the Swachh Bharat mission, saving electricity, developing children's personalities during their summer holidays, inspiring them to choose good careers, learning to avoid gender discrimination, using more khadi, etc. That's why the PM lives in old and young people's minds.

Indians took a step to build a new India that can walk with the world. The country firmly believes and trusts in Narendra Modi's leadership, which they saw at work in this short three-year period.

CHAPTER TEN

Modi's New India

The achievements of Prime Minister Narendra Modi in the last four years have been amazingly important for India. India is now recognized as the fastest growing economy in the world, from foreign policy to poor infrastructure schemes. India is punching over her weight for the first time in decades. The leaders of the world recognize this and the Indians. India isolated Pakistan as a state in which terrorists are nurtured and sent to the military establishment to fight proxy wars. Each document that emerged from a strategic meeting with the US, Europe, China and Russia highlighted terrorist groups from Pakistan. Even the Middle East countries are squarely behind India. During Doklam, Modi was tough on China and the Surgical Strike against Pakistan was a bold and decisive move to let Pakistan know that it was not' business as usual.'

PM Modi has managed to balance India's needs with Iran and Russia, although the US has both endorsed them. However, Iran's Chabahar is fully functional and India will have Russia's latest missile defense system. That's no bad thing. India has become the strongest ally of America in South Asia at the same time. As regards economic growth ratesY, India's growth rate will be around 7.4% in 2018 and

7.8% in 2019, according to an IMF report. India's economy "lifts from strong private consumption and fading transitional effects of the currency exchange initiative and the implementation of the national tax on goods and services," the report notes. "in the medium term, it is expected that growth will gradually increase with the continued implementation of structural reforms that increase productivity and encourage private investment."

In a recent interview, Anand Mahindra said Modi's greatest achievement is to change mindsets. The PM has tried to change the mindset of more than a billion people, from digital payments to taxes, to work toward the end of open defecation, which led to millions of children dying before the age of five, and women's insecurity about going to fields at night. In a short period of four years, more than 450 million Indians have stopped defecating in the open thanks to government-aided toilets. It can be remembered when Modi said as a PM candidate, "We need to build more toilets rather than temples."

It was an amazingly open admission and that day it is realized that India had a man who would make every effort to do what was best for India, regardless of the odds. We didn't realize how many dreams and deadlines were fulfilled, we'd see in the next five years.

Bill Gates was impressed with what had been achieved in this area in 2017 and said that when he first heard about the vision of PM Modi, he doubted that it could be done so quickly. It was India's shame and thinking that this task was undertaken on a war basis and achieved shows how much can be done if there is' political will.' If only the Congress had given the Gandhian vision of cleanliness in the 1960s as godliness, in the 21st century we wouldn't have had to deal with it.

By linking Aadhar to people's bank accounts and verifying the status of subsidy recipients, one million poor people disappeared in Maharashtra as fraudsters; more than 30 million fake holders of LPG connections have ended; one million, ninety-five thousand children who did not exist and received scholarships from the madrasas have disappeared; more than 1.5 million fake holders of ration cards have been scrapped. In the last two years, 50 million people have emerged from poverty and around Rs 900,000 million have been saved by eliminating fraudulent beneficiaries.

Furthermore, the tax authorities are scrutinizing 1.7 million suspect account holders with sudden windfalls due to demonetization. As Arun Jaitley rightly pointed out, "monetary confiscation was not a demonetization objective. The broader objective was to get it into the formal economy and to make the holders pay tax. "There was also a steep increase in digital payments, with digital platforms such as UPI and Rupay cards developed indigenously. Income tax collections were 20 percent higher and collections of corporate taxes were 19.5 percent higher in 2018/2019 until 31 September 2018 compared to the previous year. It also led to the closure of shell companies ' lakhs and huge decreases in real estate black money.

India's corruption is so endemic that it won't end by waving a magic wand, but it needs a change of mindset and PM Modi had the vision to act, even though he knew it wouldn't be popular with his electoral base, something no other politician would have done. GST also helped to rationalize the taxes paid for goods transported at various stages. The economy was formalized and thetaxpayerr base increased from 6.4 million to 12 million.

Another promise PM Modi kept was to work on India's ease of doing business. According to the latest annual World Bank ratings, India is ranked 77 among 190 economies in the ease of doing business. India's rank improved from 100 in 2017 to 77 in 2018. Business facility in India averaged 124.82 from 2008 to 2018, reaching an all-time high of 139 in 2010 and a record low of 77 in 2018. PM Modi, however, has set his sight on putting India under 50 in the index and India will achieve it after another five years.

Cisco's former CEO John Chambers said he met many world leaders, but Modi was amazing and had a clear vision for India. Cisco's CEO Chuck Robbins said India's digitalization pace is unparalleled under Modi. He said in an interview with Times of India: "Every country does unique things. But when you look broadly at the efforts of Skills India and Smart Cities, the UID Card, and what JIO is doing to bring broadband connectivity to people at a price that wasn't conceivable-I think the rate of digitization that flows into the population to businesses is perhaps unparalleled all over the world.

The Center has also focused on facilitating the business environment for start-ups, removing regulatory barriers for msmes and building infrastructural platforms to facilitate technology solutions. More than $40 billion has been poured into the Indian startup ecosystem in this environment since 2014. The high level of investment underlines the confidence of global and domestic investors.

Every village in India had access to electricity in April last year. This means that all 597,464 villages inhabited by the country now have access to power. On 15 August 2015, PM Modi announced that all non-electrified villages would receive power over the next 1000 days and delivered. Although the villages have the power infrastructure, households now have to apply for a connection and state governments have to ensure supply. Another major focus was to supply poor women with cooking gas. After being raised in a poor household, Modi knew how wood and coal smoke affected poor women during cooking. Since the government came to power, it has distributed 100 million LPG connections in four years, including 40 million free of charge, to poor women, 45% of whom were Dalits and tribals, resulting in a "great social transformation."

PM Modi achieved a number of milestones in just the first 48 months, including Jan Dhan Yojna, in which poor people opened 310 million bank accounts and deposited Rs 800,000 million. The government paid a loan of Rs 4.5

billion under the Mudra Yojna, while the Pradhan Mantri Krishi Sinchai Yojana helped to eliminate the problem of water scarcity in farmland.

Pradhan Mantri Fasal Beema Yojana: Launched in 2016, it compensates farmers for any loss in crop yields. E-NAM portal connecting farmers to buyers on an online trading commodity platform. E-rakam 2017 portal, which allows farmers to sell their agricultural yield online; neem-coated urea prevents farmers from entering other sectors; crop insurance schemes have been initiated to help farmers in the event of drought.

For bovine breeding and dairy development, the Rashtriya Gokul Mission was launched. Its objective is the organized and scientific preservation and propagation of indigenous breeds. Furthermore, agricultural institutions have been linked to providing information to farmers about the soil on which they grow crops and what is the best crop to grow under the conditions in their areas.

On the infrastructure front, the speed of road construction has increased from just 2 kilometers a day to 28 kilometers and in the coming year it will be accelerated to build 40-45 kilometers a day. In addition, the Delhi Ring Road and the 14-lane expressway Delhi-Meerut were inaugurated. Work has begun on the Dwarka Expressway and the Mumbai Vadodara Expressway, which are mega projects of Rs 7000 crore and Rs 44000 crore. Work on the road to Char Dham has also begun.

The work on inland waterways began for the first time after India's independence and the Center is working on 10 inland waterways. In fact, the 20,000 km long river will be transformed into waterways. In addition, profits are running at 12 major ports. Profits were at Rs 3000 crore in the first year, at Rs 4000 crores in the next year, at Rs 5000 crore in 2016, and in 2017, profits increased to Rs 7000 crores. The PM inaugurated the largest bridge built in India a few months ago, which will reduce the distance from Assam to Arunachal from 600 km to 40 km. At record speed, highways are being built connecting all parts of India.

One Rank One Pension cannot be omitted, it was something that Veterans had long overdue, and Modi kept his campaign promise. There are several other beneficial schemes that transform our landscape and bring about change in all walks of life for people. It would take several pages to describe what the current government has achieved in detail. Anyone interested can go to the My Gov.in portal to see what has happened in every part of India and give suggestions on what they want to do further.

Swachh Bharat must be the favorite programs, as much else can be achieved, such as increased tourism and better health, with an emphasis on clean India. Another was when I had to sell a flat after demonetization and when I heard the words, "We're going to pay all the check," it was music to my ears. I knew no other way I had lived abroad for 20 years! From seeing cleaner and more user-friendly railway stations to clean trains, to roads that have suddenly appeared in the last four years, to transparency and easy bill payments and electricity 24/7. What a difference 56 months made and how quickly they flew.

Opportunities for growth and transformation

India could create sustainable economic conditions in five ways, such as promoting acceptable standards of living, improving urban infrastructure and unlocking women's potential.

Modi-fied India

India embarked on an economic liberalization journey twenty-five years ago, opening its doors to globalization and market forces. India and the rest of the world have watched the investment and trade regime introduced in 1991 increase economic growth, increase the choice of consumers and significantly reduce poverty.

The International Monetary Fund has now projected that India's GDP will grow by 7.4 percent in 2016-17, making it the fastest-growing large economy in the world, as uncertainties cloud the global economic picture. India also compares its growth potential favorably with other emerging markets. The country offers 89 million households by 2025 an attractive long-term future powered by a consumer class that is expected to more than triple.

Liberalization has created new possibilities. The challenge for policymakers is to manage growth so that sustainable economic performance is based on it. Although much work has been done, the transformation of India into a global economic force has not yet been fully beneficial to all its citizens. Basic services such as water and sanitation, energy and health care, for example, are massively unmet, while bureaucracy makes it difficult to do business. Many of these challenges have been addressed by the government, and the pace of change may accelerate in the coming years as some initiatives gain in scale.

Modi-fied India

India has an exciting future from a point of view. India's rise is reported in the new mckinsey Global Institute: We look at five opportunities for growth and transformation for the country's economy and the implications for domestic companies, multinationals and government. There is no comprehensive assessment of India's prospects in the five areas we focus on, but we believe that they are among the most important trends. Foreign and Indian companies would do well to recognize these opportunities and to think about how they can be exploited.

From poverty to empowerment: Acceptable living standards for all

The trickle-down effect of economic liberalisation, in the last two decades, has lifted millions of Indians out of poverty. The official poverty rate decreased from 45 percent of the population in 1994 to 22 percent in 2012, but only the most dismal situations are defined in this statistics. By our broader measure of minimum acceptable living standards-nutrition, water, sanitation, energy, housing, education and health-in 2012 56 percent of Indians lacked the basics.

In order to achieve its potential, the country will need to address these gaps. The task is certainly within India's capacity, but policymakers will need to promote an agenda that emphasizes job creation, growth-oriented investment, productivity in the farm sector and innovative social programs that help people who really need them. The private sector plays a significant role in the creation and delivery of effective basic services.

Sustainable urbanization: Building India's growth engines

India will have 69 cities with a population of more than one million by 2025, according to MGI estimates. Economic growth will focus on them and there will be the largest infrastructure building. Indian cities ' output will resemble cities in middle-income countries. In 2030, for example, the economy of Mumbai, a mammoth consumption market of

$245 billion, will be larger than today's Malaysia. The next four market-sized cities will each consume $80 billion to $175 billion annually by 2030.

These cities must become more livable places, offering clean air and water, reliable utilities and extensive green spaces in order to achieve sustainable growth. India's urban transformation represents an enormous opportunity for domestic and international companies that can provide know-how in terms of capital, technology and planning, as well as the demand for goods and services from urban consumers.

Manufacturing for India, in India

While India's manufacturing sector lags behind China's, there will be significant opportunities to invest in value-creating companies and create jobs. India's appeal to potential investors will be more than just its low-cost labor: There are manufacturers who build competitive companies to tap into the large and growing local market. Further reforms and investments in public infrastructure could facilitate scale and efficiency for all types of manufacturing companies, both foreign and Indian.

Riding the digital wave: Harnessing technology for India's growth

Twelve powerful technologies will benefit India, helping to increase productivity, improve efficiency in key economic sectors and radically change the provision of services such as education and healthcare. According to our analysis, these technologies could add $550 billion to $1 trillion per year of economic value in 2025, potentially creating millions of well-paid, productive jobs (including jobs for people with moderate levels of formal education) and helping millions of Indians enjoy decent living standards.

Unlocking the potential of Indian women: If not now, when?

Research suggests that women now account for only 17 percent of India's GDP and only 24 percent of the workforce, compared to 40 percent worldwide. They will be one of the country's largest potential economic forces in the coming decade. If it matched the region's most rapidly improving country's progress towards gender parity, we estimate it could add $700 billion to its GDP in 2025. Movement has begun to close the gender gap in education and financial and digital inclusion, but further progress can be made.

Efforts are underway in the public sector to address the five areas. The government is trying to improve the investment climate and accelerate the creation of jobs-India's ranking in the Global Competitiveness Report of the World Economic Forum increased from 71 a year earlier to 55 in 2015-16. Officials move to make the government more efficient by using technology that can overcome traditional weak infrastructure bottlenecks. For example, one billion Indian citizens are now registered under Aadhaar, the largest digital identity program in the world, and a powerful platform for directly benefiting the poor.

In fulfilling India's promise, national, state and local leaders will need to adopt new approaches to governance and service provision. These officials will also need new skills to meet the aspirations of the people. The requirements include expertise in the procurement and supply chain style of the private sector, profound technical skills in planning infrastructure investment portfolios, and strong project management capabilities in order to ensure that large capital projects are completed on time and on budget. Training will be needed to help employees use digital technologies to automate and re-engineer processes, manage big data and advanced analytics, and improve citizens ' interactions through digitized contact points, online access platforms, portals, messaging and payment platforms. The government could acquire these capabilities by adopting quality-oriented procurement policies and using private sector assignments. India represents a large market for businesses, but requires a granular strategy and a local operating model.

No single report can capture all the changes in the country, but we have tried to identify the most important trends here. Foreign and Indian companies should consider how they influence their strategies. Policymakers should focus on helping to capitalize on all stakeholders. The challenge is daunting by any measure, but success could give India's economy a historic boost.

CHAPTER ELEVEN

Agricultural Reform Under Modi

Narendra Modi was sworn in four years ago as India's prime minister in the midst of the kind of excitement and expectation that has not been seen in decades. A single party won an electoral majority not for 30 years. The success of Modi, his rhetoric and background all seemed to be a decisive break from India's past -one that many Indians wanted to embrace. What exactly was Modi expected? That's certainly a fair way to judge how his government has done a bid for re-election next year. As far as economic policy is concerned -where the previous Congress administration was most disappointed -voters hoped to see three things: less corruption, greater policy-making decisiveness and more market-friendly reform.

Even critics of Modi must admit -and welcome -that he has made real progress on all three. However, even his fans must recognize that his government has not lived up to its potential, given its advantages. Under PM Narendra Modi, the NDA government has placed unprecedented emphasis on agriculture. Many initiatives have been taken to improve productivity, protect farmers and increase their incomes and improve their overall well-being.

The government of PM Narendra Modi has set a goal to double farm incomes by 2022 and is working to achieve the same with multi-modal focus. The focus was on reforms throughout the agricultural cycle, from seeds and soil to market access. There is also a renewed focus on related activities to help farmers' incomes. First of all, the NDA government has record budget allocations for agriculture and farmers' welfare. The government of PM Narendra Modi allocated Rs 2,11,694 crore in the 2014-19 period compared to the previous government tenure from 2009 to 2014, which saw an allocation of Rs 1,21,082 crore. This is almost twice as much.

In order to ensure good yields for the farmer, it is imperative to focus on strengthening sowing-related activities. In this respect, the government has taken various steps. Since soil health plays a key role in agriculture, from 2015 to 2018, the government has sent more than 13 crore soil health cards. Soil Health Cards contain crop-specific nutrient and fertilizer recommendations to help farmers improve their productivity.

There are hardly any state complaints about the distribution of fertilizers. The reason for this is the significant increase in Urea production, since the government has revived the deceased fertilizer plants and also established new plants. Since the government implemented Urea's 100 percent neem coating, it not only improved the quality of the soil, but also prevented fertilizers from being diverted to other uses. A special arrangement for the clearance of fertilizer subsidy is Rs 10,000 crore.

Pradhan Mantri Krishi Sinchai Yojana is in place to ensure "more crop per drop" covering 28.5 lakh of irrigated area. Rs 50,000 crore have been set aside to ensure that every farm gets water. Rs 5,000 crore funds have been made available for micro-irrigation while farmers have been encouraged to install solar pumps for irrigation.

Credit for farmers

The Modi Government has taken important policy initiatives to address the issue of farm credit and to prevent farmers from being exploited by informal sources of credit, such as money lenders. Pradhan Mantri Fasal Bima Yojana is the government's largest risk and safety net. Short-term crop loans under the interest subsidy scheme up to 3 lakh with an annual interest rate of 7 percent up to one year.

Marketing the farmers produce

The government's policy follows the next logical step after supporting the farmer at the time of seeding, which helps farmers get the right price for their products. In July 2018, the government approved the historic increase in the MSP for Kharif crops to 1.5 times the cost, which will give farmers a 50 percent profit margin over production costs.

The national agricultural market scheme known as e-NAM has integrated 585 markets in 16 countries and 2 territories of the Union. More than 164.53 tons of agricultural commodities were transacted by e-NAM and more than 87 lakh farmers were registered. It is therefore cutting agricultural trade intermediaries to facilitate farmers with their due. 22,000 rural haats will become the Gramin Agriculture Market, benefiting 86 percent of small farmers. Large investments in warehousing and cold chains to prevent losses of crops after harvest and added value through food processing also provide farmers with an essential market edge. "Operation Greens" has been put in place to address the price volatility of perishable items such as tomato, potato and onion.

Focus on allied sectors

As noted earlier, the focus was on related agricultural activities to increase the income of farmers. Corpus of Rs 10,000 crore established to create fishing, aquaculture and animal husbandry infrastructure. Integrated fisheries development and management with a cost of Rs 3000 crore, the establishment of 20 Gokul Grams are some of the examples in this respect.

Growth in production

There is ample evidence that the implementation of agricultural policy by PM Narendra Modi has yielded results. With 279.51 million tons of food grain production, agricultural production reached a new high in 2017-18. The pulses buffer stock rose from 1.5 lakh tons to 20 lakh tons. Production of milk in 2016-17 increased by 18.81 percent compared to 2013-14. In keeping with the spirit of

Modi-fied India

PM Narendra Modi's motto -Beej se le ke Bazaar tak -the
government has pursued a holistic approach to agriculture
and positive results have begun to shine on the ground

Under the guidance of Honorable Prime Minister Shri
Narendra Modi, enthusiastic and positive results are
visible from sustained efforts to improve agriculture and
farmers. The government of Modi is committed to
farmers' welfare. As a result of this, their lives have
improved qualitatively. Modi's government has set new
transparency standards for the country's development.
Under the leadership of the Prime Minister, the
government has transformed the objectives intended to
implement farmers' welfare schemes in a mission mode
and time-limited manner. Our government has established
a modern and future-oriented India with new dimensions,
innovations and a reformist approach to good governance.
Modi's government has succeeded in raising awareness
among farmers through new initiatives for the
development of the country's agricultural sector. During
this tenure, a concerted and strong effort has been made
to bring about qualitative changes in farmers' and rural
lives.

Dr Swaminathan, President of the National Commission on
Farmers (NCF), informed the then government in his

report in 2006 that proper attention should be paid to the well-being of farmers and agro-based thinking. Farmers give an important direction to economic reform efforts. Therefore, proper emphasis should be placed on post-harvest marketing and related arrangements in order to make radical changes to the system. The Agriculture Commission also called for attention to the management of natural resources based on science and sustainable production and development, taking into account the unabated erosion of natural resources and climate change.

In his article published in the Times of India on 6 August 2018, Dr. Swaminathan said: "Although the NCF report was submitted in 2006, very little action was taken until the current government headed by Prime Minister Narendra Modi took office. Fortunately, several important decisions have been taken over the last four years to improve the status and income of farmers." The government has taken a number of initiatives for the development of the agricultural sector, remunerative returns for the production of farmers and reducing production costs. These efforts have led to significant changes in their lives. An important aspect of this thought is the establishment of the national soil health card scheme.

The government made the use of neem-coated urea mandatory to reduce agricultural costs and increase the competence of the nitrogen utility. Since it has led to increased productivity, thereby reducing agricultural costs, it has also helped to prevent its abuse in the non-agricultural sector. Paramparagat Krishi Vikas Yojana (PMKY) has been linked to organic farming for sustained agricultural development and soil health, including in-situ rice straw management. The Pradhan Mantri Krishi Sinchayee Yojana (PMKSY) is a very important scheme for the proper management of water in agriculture. The world's largest farmer-friendly Pradhan Mantri Fasal Bima Yojna and Weather-based crop insurance scheme was initiated in 2016 after a comprehensive study of the previous schemes and reformed them. These schemes provide extensive coverage of all risks in the agricultural sector.

The National Farmers Commission made a number of recommendations to increase farmers' income. With these recommendations in mind, the government has implemented many reform plans. The government released to all states the 2016 Model Agricultural Land Leasing Act, which is a very important step in agricultural reforms. Both the landowners and the lease recipient's interests are protected. Implementation of market reforms has led to increased market transparency. The e-NAM scheme links the country's agricultural markets. In addition to the country's 585 mandates, the government also established the national agricultural market by focusing on open trade between the mandates. The 2018 budget highlighted the much-needed new structure for marketing. The government has also made arrangements to sell their products to small and marginal farmers in nearby markets. The country has 22,000 rural markets, reducing the gap between them. Small and marginal farmers can effectively sell their products while linking with APMC and e-Nam. By establishing rural agricultural markets, farmers can sell their products directly to consumers or retailers and receive compensatory prices. The Modi government has formulated and published a model "Agricultural Product and Livestock Marketing Act 2016" in order to achieve a strong and competent agricultural market with a proper judicial framework. In addition, the Agriculture Production and Livestock Contract Farming and Services Act, 2018, was sent to States for adoption.

The decision to provide MSP with a production cost of 50 percent and more is an important step for farmers. The government is also committed to MSP. The procurement was confined to paddy and wheat since the start of the

Green Revolution. Sometimes other commodities were also procured. After the Modi government took charge, the procurement of pulses and oilseeds was tremendously improved. We are determined to extend profits to the farmers of pulses, oilseeds, coarse cereals etc through the State Governments. By procuring these crops at MSP, the benefits will be extended to farmers who have long been deprived. These crops are climate-oriented and tolerant of future climate change. The Honorable Prime Minister set the goal of doubling farmers' income in 2022 for the 75th year of independence. The government provides a new direction to determine the minimum price of support and to provide assured returns, including equality and the welfare of farmers. Dr. Swaminathan recently said in his article published in the Times of India on 6 August 2018: "The recent announcement of a remunerative price based mainly on the NCF recommendation is a very important step in ensuring the economic viability of agriculture. In its notification, the government has ensured that the MSP of the notified crops will be at least 150 percent of the production costs from Kharif 2018; it ranges from 150 to 200 percent for coarse cereals."

The government also emphasizes livestock, fisheries and the development of water bodies in addition to agriculture. The Rashtriya Gokul Mission is an integral part of the overall development of the agricultural sector, based on the conservation and development of indigenous bovine species. This will benefit many small and marginal farmers, including landless farmers who own these indigenous bovine species. It is a matter of great pride that 161 indigenous species have been registered throughout the country and that ICAR is actively working for this purpose. The development of the development of fish production, including sea and freshwater fish, improves the lives of the fishing community. Fish production has achieved a higher rate of growth than all other agricultural sectors.

For small farmers who cannot earn enough income for their families, they promote related farming. Government collaborative agricultural schemes include beekeeping, mushroom production, agricultural forestry and bamboo production, etc. The production of agricultural natural resources will help to create additional jobs and income in agriculture. In the light of the National Commission on Farmers' recommendations to increase productivity and eliminate malnutrition, the ICAR has developed a total of 795 improved crop varieties in the last four years, of which 495 are climate-tolerant. They were handed over to farmers to take advantage of these advanced varieties. For the first time, the government has taken a historic initiative to overcome the long-standing problem of malnutrition in Indian society. 20 bio-fortified varieties have been developed and released for cultivation. 45 models of the Integrated Farming System (IFS) have been developed to increase the income of families of marginal and small farmers. This will help to improve soil health, increase the efficiency of water use and conserve biodiversity in agriculture. These models have been found to be beneficial in different states in terms of economic evaluation. This model is set up and displayed in each KVK to help farmers to adopt it by looking at its success and thus helping them earn more income.

Adequate budget is provided to implement policy reforms and new agricultural schemes. The government of Modi has taken measures in recent years to implement and strengthen these schemes and a budgetary provision of Rs 2.11.694 crore has been made. In addition, the government has created corpus funds to improve milk, cooperative, fisheries and aquaculture infrastructure, animal husbandry, agricultural markets and micro irrigation. In view of the welfare of agriculture, farmers and consumers, the government has adopted an income-oriented approach to sustainable production.

Prime Minister Narendra Modi has set a target of doubling farmers' incomes by 2022 in order to improve the economic condition of farmers. A prime minister has put forward a target for the overall well-being of farmers for the first time in the country. In accordance with this vision, the Ministry of Agriculture and Farmers' Welfare will adopt a concrete strategy, based on the recommendations of the established committee, in order to achieve the objective of doubling farmers' incomes by August 2022, when our country celebrates the 75th Independence Day. The results are also visible.

CHAPTER TWELVE

Modi deserves a second term!

"No" and "Yes".

If you can show a better opposition PM candidate who can provide a stable government with positive policies for India, which is likely to reach somewhere between 225-300 seats, Narendra Modi may automatically be out of the picture, and in 2019 he would not deserve a second term. But there's no opposition leader in the present scenario who can do that.

Congress is the only opposition party in the range of 50-100 seats in elections in 2019. But it's not enough to give a stable and honest government. Remember Manmohan Singh's words when he was PM in the UPA coalition government, showing his alliance policy compulsion? So much so that by calling it a compulsion he even justified corruption by allies?

In addition, Congress leader Rahul Gandhi is still a politically mature person. Of course, in the last one or two years, his image has changed. But it didn't get better. It's just changed. He was previously regarded as a naive person. He's considered a person who can speak lies without his eyes blinking. His declared policies (including free promises), if he assumes power, do not inspire much confidence in a possible good governance.

Other than Congress, other opposition leaders may not be able to cross the figure for their individual parties of 30 or 40 seats in Lok Sabha (Talking about their individual party tallies, not the opposition as a whole). This is simply because none of the other opposition parties would contest more than approximately 40 seats. Even if they win 100 percent, they cannot cross the figure of 30 or 40 seats individually. All other parties are regional parties or national parties in more than one or two states with a limited presence.

Mamata Banerjee, for example, does not exist outside West Bengal. Akhilesh Yadav does not exist outside U.P. Mayawati's main stake is in U.P., although in a few other states she has some minor stakes. The JD (S) of Deve Gowda is out of Karnataka nowhere. Chandrababu Naidu has no chance outside Andhra Pradesh (and in Telangana to some extent). Stalin won't compete outside Tamil Nadu (and in Puducherry, too, maybe one seat). Naveen Patnaik is limited to Odisha alone. KCR is in Telangana alone. Sharad Pawar's NCP is mainly in Maharashtra. And so is Uddhav Thackeray's Shiv Sena. Lalu Yadav is in Bihar alone.

CPM / CPI and other communist parties are now confined mostly to Kerala only (and, may be getting a few seats in West Bengal, or one or two seats in Tripura).

The AAP of Arvind Kejriwal is mostly limited to Delhi and Punjab. His party can also compete in a couple of seats in other states, but mostly to lose deposit. Is there any other party that I didn't consider having any influence? Maybe it will be AIADMK and Akali Dal. But they're likely to be BJP's alliance partners.

None of these opposition parties (other than Congress, which have already been discussed) are likely to receive more than 30 or 40 seats, since they are mostly confined to individual states and the number of seats in which they are contested would be within this range.

Can their leaders provide a stable government for five years at the Centre? And, too, with positive India policies? I'm sorry about that. I think it's not possible. We've seen how the government alliance works.

So if you can show some opposition leader who can provide a better stable government for five years and positive policies for India than Narendra Modi, then it can be agreed that Modi does not deserve to be PM because there is a better alternative. But if there's no better alternative, then what?

Then, of course, Modi deserves at least one more chance to lead India. India need a stable government that has positive or at least neutral policies. Indians don't want someone who has totally negative policies or can't provide a reasonably stable government.

If a single party cannot obtain an absolute majority, it can be agreed that the alliance of parties is the only option. But it is also advisable if one party receives at least 200+ seats to offer at least a semblance of stability. It would not be in national interests to have a complete khichdi (here, meaning, messy, untidy, dirty) government.

Democracy means that by election, people have the right to choose their leader. Election means selecting one candidate from many contesting candidates. Election should therefore elect the best candidate possible. This is, of course, according to the collective choice of people, not in absolute terms.

Therefore, if there is a better alternative to Modi (you can put that forward), then the PM deserves to be such a better alternative. But if there is no better alternative than Modi, he deserves to be the PM again in 2019 because the people, the ultimate sovereign in India, would elect him.

Now, from a different perspective, to answer the above question. Who and I decide if Modi deserves a second term as PM? The Indian people must decide by casting their individual votes, acting collectively. If people choose to vote for Modi, he deserves to be PM and no one can cast him out. But if people choose to vote for someone else (individual or party), Modi would of course be out of PM's post. So, the answer must come from the Indian people. There are about 91 crore voters who will decide to answer this question collectively. Whatever you say, it's just an academic exercise. Yet, even if it's an academic answer, there's a feeling that Modi's current political environment will win the 2019 election.

Fifteen reasons why Narendra Modi deserves a second term

The bugle was blown with the interim electoral budget for the 2019 Lok Sabha campaign. Although a budget cannot win over or convert the majority of the voters to one's side, it was necessary to have a good budget to start the re-election campaign on the right note. Although the interim budget targeted the main constituency of small and marginal farmers, unorganized labor (which earned less than 15,000 per month) and lower middle class and young taxpayers, it was only an icing on the cake. Modi's government is not just fighting on budget announcements for the 2019 elections. In this five-year term, they have many achievements to show.

Reasons why Modi deserves a second term

Returned the economy from the precipice: In May 2014, India's economy was considered one of the world's five fragile economies. With every minister concerned and ally looting, the UPA II government was an unmitigated disaster as there was no tomorrow. They knew they didn't return. Unlike Indian politicians who don't want to reveal that they want the coveted post, Modi run the campaign wanting to be prime minister. The rate of GDP growth decreased, inflation rose steadily, especially food inflation. The Indian economy, which was cut five years later in 2019, is doing well despite the global slowdown. Indeed, India has been China's most rapidly growing major economy in the last two years. Inflation is just above 2% and growth is projected to be around 7.2%. Modi has done many things that have caused this turnaround. In the points below, many of these actions are covered.

Resusticating the banking system: The UPA II government wrecked the banking system with its "Phone-a-Loan" facility. Company promoters have loans as never before. They built up capacities that even 5-10 years later demand would not match. In fact, the money was available from the banks so cheaply that many businessmen took loans to build non-core companies. The banks have always greened the bad loans in order to prevent them from becoming non-performing assets (NPAs) in bank books. Banks have suffered as a result of increasing NPAs and their lending capacity has been severely impeded. Small companies found the credit tap had passed away. The Modi government and the RBI began to correct the mess from here. The banks were forced to carry out a bank loan audit and the staggering amount of bank NPAs came out of the closet. Banks have to write off these bad loans that let the poison out of the system. Due to this audit, many scams such as the PNB scam came to light. The Indian Bankruptcy Code (IBC) was enacted and the National Company Law Tribunal (NCLT) was responsible for dealing with the problem of bad loans. The NCLT received major loans accounts and many of these cases were resolved or on the verge of resolution. But IBC's real benefit is not recovery of bad loans (in some cases with minimal or no hair cuts). The real benefit is that the promoters are concerned that they would lose their business in the subsequent insolvency proceedings if they do not repay the loan on time. Promoters urge banks not to refer their case to NCLT and payment of outstanding loans has been picked up. The point is that the Modi Govt and the RBI have institutionalized bad loan recovery in the form of IBC.

Clean up national resource allocation process: The UPA government lost its credibility due to massive corruption in the auction of national resources such as coal mines, 2G spectrum and 3G spectrum, etc. Coal mines have been distributed as gift boxes for Diwali. The 2G spectrum was also given to companies such as Unitech and DB Realty etc., which were not even in the telecommunications business. The Supreme Court immediately threw the gauntlet at the Modi government by canceling the coal mines allocation. By re-auctioning the coal mines through a transparent auction process, Modi's government turned the challenge into an opportunity. For the telecommunications spectrum, similar auction process was also used.

Bridging the multi-decade governance deficit: Modi's government had to address several gaps in governance in worldly areas, such as providing sanitation coverage that was only 45% in 2014. Modi was probably the first toilet prime minister. Swachh Bharat andolan first targeted the lack of toilets that gave people, especially women, better health, safety and dignity. Modi's government electrified 17,000 non-electrified villages and Saubhagya yojana is on track to electrify nearly all India's willing non-electrified houses. The Jan Dhan scheme corrected the banking system's omission of poor citizens. The benefits of these accounts have been realized by the PSU banks that complained about unprofitable zero balance accounts. Bank accounts enabled health and accident insurance to be provided, and created the credit history needed to obtain bank credit. PM Awas Yojana helped to build 1.5 crore houses for the poor and is moving towards fulfilling the shelter guarantee for everyone by 2020. PM Ujjwala Yojana helped 6 poor households to get gas cylinders to cook without smoke. This was a major revolution in empowering women and in the next two years the scheme will meet its target of eight crore gas connections.

Health for everyone: The government of Modi has unleashed a health care revolution. The government has taken several steps, such as opening approximately 3600 +

Jan Aushadi stores throughout the country that offer cheaper generic medicine. The cost of coronary stents and knee implants was reduced by up to 70%, making them affordable for the common man (and woman). Mission Indradhanush was implemented and involved vaccinating children under the age of two years and pregnant women for deadly diseases such as rubella, Japanese encephalitis (the disease wrecked by Gorakhpur, but now largely controlled), rotavirus, etc. The most far-reaching reform, however, was the Ayushman Bharat scheme, which provides free medical care for ten crore poor families up to 5 lakhs per year. According to the Socio Economic Caste Census (SECC), approximately 40 crore of the country's poorest citizens. This scheme covered routine procedures such as cataracts and cesareans for complex procedures such as heart bypass or cancer treatment. More than 10 lakh patients received free treatment in the first 135 days of the scheme. This scheme could be a benchmark for world governments with Director-General Tedros Adhanom Ghebreyesus of the World Health Organization (WHO) and the billionaire philanthropist Bill Gates praised the scheme. Ayushman Bharat will also increase capacity in private medical facilities, as approximately 60 percent of patients used private hospital facilities.

Increased road and rail infrastructure: This is one area that requires little writing. Nitin Gadkari's efforts as minister of surface transport have increased the rate of road construction from 2 km / day to 27 km / day. In the last two years, many of the Marquee road projects have been completed. The road network of the village has been expanded as never before. One of Gadkari's key successes was to raise resources outside the budget allocation. After review, all pending road projects have been financially resolved or terminated. Innovation such as the hybrid annuity model has helped to close many projects financially. Earlier and later by Mr. Piyush Goyal, railways saw a huge leap under Mr. Suresh Prabhu. Due to the Modi government's efforts, many North East states came to the railway map for the first time. Railway electrification has been accelerated and bottlenecks in the rail network have been resolved, such as at the junction of Pandit Deen Dayal Upadhyaya (formerly Mughalsarai). High-speed semi-trains such as Train 18 "Made in India" are sure to revolutionize rail travel. The planned bullet train route from Mumbai to Ahmedabad will add another feather to the Indian railway cap. Stations and trains' cleanliness has made railways a little user-friendly.

Common citizens fly high with UDAN: In the UPA years, aviation has always been regarded as a mode of travel for the wealthy or a sector plagued by several scams. Through the Ude Desh ka Aam Nagrik (UDAN), the NDA government was able to create an explosion in traffic to small towns. Approximately 100 under-used airports have been connected via short 1-hour flights. New airports have been built, such as the amazing Pakyong airport in Sikkim and Sindhudurg's Chipi airport in Maharashtra. Many new airports, such as Navi Mumbai, Pune and Jewar, are under construction. Half of the tickets for each flight are subsidized under UDAN and the price is limited to Rs. 2,500 for less than 1 hour. This helps small towns to grow business or improve tourist footfalls in heritage sites such as Hampi or temple towns such as Shirdi. The government was able to avoid any scams and did not avoid protecting private airlines such as UPA. The aviation sector will be very important as India moves towards an economy of $10 trillion by 2030.

Internal Security and the harsh pursuit of terrorists: In any major city outside J&K and Punjab, there have been almost four and a half years of no bomb blasts or terrorist attacks. Shri Rajnath Singh and Mr. Kiren Rijiju can be attributed to this success. Given UPA's five annual blasts in almost all India's states, this is a welcome change. Much has been improved on the intelligence apparatus. NSA Ajit Doval played an enormous role in the background. There has also been a hard pursuit of terrorists in J&K, the removal of naxals in the red corridor (which has dramatically shrunk). To eliminate terrorists, the government has given the army a free hand. The commander of terrorist posts such as Hizbul Mujahideen and Lashkar saw the incumbent last at best a couple of days or a month before he was eliminated. The surgical strike in PoK and Myanmar was undoubtedly the highlight. India had previously carried out a kilometer of enemy territory with local strikes. But the surgical strike after Uri and Myanmar took place far deeper and devastatingly in enemy territory. While the Indian army was always able to strike in the enemy territory, the Modi government allowed them to plan and strike as they thought appropriate.

Increased tax ratio to GDP and low inflation: UPA II ended up with 11% inflation and 4.5% growth. Modi's government first worked to heal and then strengthen the economy. The growth rate in 2019 is 7.2% and inflation is just over 2% (within the 4% tolerance level of the RBI

Monetary Policy Committee). Steps such as malignant demonetization and GST contributed to the direct income tax collection from 6.38 lakh crore (FY 2013-14) to 12 lakh crore (FY 2018-19). The new indirect tax regime in the form of GST is stabilizing successfully and the average monthly collection is improving to 95,000 crore and is expected to continue to strengthen. India has always had the best tax-to-GDP ratio. Lower inflation indirectly means savings for households. The interim budget for sweeteners allows 80 percent of personal income taxpayers earning up to 7-8 lakh a year to pay zero income tax (with some investment). 10 percent reserve for economically weaker sections: Providing an economic reserve of 10 percent for economically weaker families among Hindu upper castes and unreserved people of other religions in educational institutions and government jobs is a step in the right direction. This was done without affecting the SC/ST and OBC communities' existing 50 percent reservation. The real thing is that government reservations and private educational institutions will help poor children in the unreserved communities. Going to the college of choice will help to qualify for public or lucrative jobs in the private sector. On economically weaker criteria, I suggested a 20 percent quota. Govt gave a quota of 10 percent, but made a good start.

Renewable energy growth: The government of Modi was relentless in its pursuit of 225 GW of renewable energy by

2022. In fact, the target was revised upwards from the initial 175 GW, as the government achieved 75 GW of renewable energy at various stages of completion with an additional 40 GW capacity. Most of this comes from solar energy and wind power. Modi led the world in the Paris Agreement and began the International Solar Alliance with France. Many experts and governments applauded this leadership in containing climate change. Renewable energy is at the heart of this change, with India targeting total migration to electric vehicles by 2030. After all, driving a non-polluting electric vehicle is useless if electricity is generated from a coal-fired power plant that is highly polluting. Initial steps have already begun, such as massive procurement of electric cars by government departments and electricity charging planning.

Clean rivers and cities: Modi's government began the Namami Gange plan with a lot of fanfare and the efforts seem to be bearing fruit from the current news reports. Most polluting companies had to install waste treatment machinery in the Ganga before discharge. Instead of dumping it directly into the river, city sewage is increasingly routed to sewage treatment plants. Zero sewage discharge is planned for November 2018 in Ganga in Varanasi. Cities are also competing to be declared the cleanest. Cities such as Indore have made significant progress in this area.

MUDRA gives wings to entrepreneurs: MUDRA was a revelation in a country where the debate was about jobs or lack of jobs. Some 12 crore beneficiaries, mostly poor people, including many women, took loans from 50,000 to 10 lakh. Many of these beneficiaries were forced to take money from private lenders who fleece them earlier. MUDRA's success was the inclusion of microfinance institutions (MFIs), which were efficient in lending under MUDRA than banks. The MUDRA loan default was only 5 percent, within acceptable limits.

Space program firing on all cylinders: Modi's government has increased support for the space program by 2021 with Gaganyaan planning to send an Indian to the moon. The government approved a budget of 10,000 crore for this manned mission. With a plethora of satellites launched, including those for foreign countries, ISRO has had a good run under the Modi government. The unmanned moon and Mars missions were very successful and whetted the appetite of ISRO for more.

Muscular foreign policy: India's foreign policy has seen a significant improvement over the years of the UPA. Modi has been excellent through his foreign travels (much criticized but proven successful), Mrs. Sushma Swaraj, General VK Singh and Mr. MJ Akbar (played a stellar role before demitting office). India's soft power has manifested itself through International Yoga Day, helping foreign governments (including the United States) to evacuate

Middle East citizens or build infrastructure for war-torn countries such as Afghanistan. The port of Chabahar and the planned port connectivity to Afghanistan demolished the string of pearls that China planned to build around India. Economic offenders such as Christian Michel, Rajiv Saxena and Deepak Talwar have been extradited from the UAE. Vijay Mallya would soon join the infamous list, as the UK Home Secretary formally signed his extradition. This was possible thanks to the Modi government's exemplary diplomacy. Imagine that the antagonistic US, Russia, Syria, the United Arab Emirates, Saudi Arabia, Egypt and Israel are all friendly to India. India has finally begun to punch over its weight, as Saudi oil minister pointed out.

In conclusion, while Modi's government has made certain misses, such as education policy, smart cities, etc., the hits are more than out of number. More importantly, Modi has demonstrated his intention to run a clean and proactive government. Many of Modi's plans to culminate in August 2022 (75th year of independence), the corrupt Mayawati, Jihadi Mamata or clown prince Rahul Gandhi are also alternatives to Modi.

Why Modi should be voted Again?

Yes, PM Modi has over-promised, showed too many big dreams to Indians and may not be able to achieve all the goals he set for the present government when he came to power. But, apart from a few setbacks, what he has achieved is something that Indians believe is unprecedented. As a fairly educated young person with a good economic and political understanding. Take a detailed study of both topics. So, just as many people say they don't see anything positive happening, this book can give you enough to make your own judgment and evaluation. And with this judgment, you can understand that the government of Modi has done a fairly good job of laying a fertile land where a bumper harvest can be produced in succession for several years. And for a government in just one term, that's no mean achievement. Especially in a complicated economic set-up inherited from his predecessors by PM Modi and his team. Let's dive into the details without further talk.

Economy and Finance

Yes, when it comes to economics and finance, Indians trust the intentions of my government. They feel they've done a lot of good, even if some of their moves have fired back. At least the incumbent government takes action and does something about the mess they have inherited. The previous establishment simply did nothing to make minor mistakes in its second term! All right, it can be said that they haven't done anything. But the point is, they didn't do enough to deserve the power and command seat. No one want that kind of government.

Reforms in the financial sector, whether the GST or the IBC (Insolvency and Bankruptcy Code), are both tremendous juggernauts that our country has long needed. This government gave them the political consensus without which someone's committee would still have studied them. Of course, it is regrettable that the GST was too hastily implemented. But it is never said that this government was perfect again. Information on ground only suggest that it's much better than its predecessors. So, it is important to appreciate it for the great feat it managed to achieve when each state was part of the decision-making process. This is cooperative federalism at its best, and this government has championed it further after the times of Atal Ji.

Financial inclusion was another major milestone that made opening a bank account the poorest of all. Now their subsidies and money from various welfare schemes go directly to their accounts without any dirty intermediaries. Many people say this was a failed drive because more than half of these accounts have a zero balance. What they often miss is that the number of created accounts exceeds 33 crores. This means that even if half of those accounts are zero-balance accounts, we still have more than 16.5 poor people joining the banking loop. For many, that may be a little thing. But that's unprecedented in my opinion.

In addition, the previous government left the economy of my country in shambles with a ballooning current-account deficit, high inflation, falling forex reserves and a shaky housing market.

As many may know, the price of a property in India consists of three components. The charge for the circle and the registry. And then there's a black part. And it's this component that's gone too high and heavily reduced under the current administration. Many don't appreciate the government enough to accomplish this. But I'm sure. Because this black component was all illegal and hidden money that is clearly anti-poorand anti-development and only favors the rich. And how was it all achieved? One of the main reasons is demonetization, another is the implementation of the RERA (Real Estate Regulation Act), while another main reason is the notification of the Benami Property Act, which means that many of those people who own these properties want to sell them as soon as possible. Demand is therefore low and supply is high, reducing the costs to what more ordinary people can afford. Big victory!

Another major achievement in the economic and financial sector, in my view, is the way in which the government has dealt with the dismantling of the heaps of npas and bad loans granted by public sector banks. Under the previous administration (UPA-1 & 2), most of these banks lost their morality in lending and lent money to cops and capitalists due to continuous political pressure, interference and corruption. And the new government found itself in a deep mess when the administration changed in May 2014. It therefore launched a crackdown on these banks and their illegal and corrupt history. Slowly, a huge pile of npas began to emerge as the incumbent government continued to push the banks through more stringent audits and checks. It was therefore revealed that our public-sector banks were in a self-deprecating lending cycle that financially destroyed them. Therefore, the Insolvency and Bankruptcy Code was brought to life to improve the state of banks. A massive recapitalization exercise was also launched (former RBI Governor Raghuram Rajan also receives a large credit for unearthing npas). Similarly, more stringent provisional clauses have been imposed on banks to keep them afloat and to recover and compensate for any losses they have suffered in the past. RBI has been empowered over the way banks work with tons of powers. Preventive and corrective action has also been initiated over 11 psbs, which is now expected to increase to 6 psbs more.

Infrastructure

When India's infrastructure is discussed, it is believed that the current establishment has fared better in every metric than almost any previous administration. Whether it's roads or ports, rivers or railways, aviation or even power, I see a big change in all these sectors. Roads and roads have never been built at a rate comparable to the current rate. The previous administration left India at 11 km of road building a day. India is 27 km a day this March and is charging for 45 km a day by March 2019.

With the exception of JNPT and Mundra (which are not public sector entities), the port sector has always been lagging. Today, Indians can actually see the loss-ridden ports profiting under the supervision of the incumbent administration, while massive road construction projects are not only awarded, but are also completed, often before the scheduled deadlines. Domestic waterways were always a pipe dream with different dprs, but nothing happened on the ground. This government got the ball rolling, pushed the policy, defined a timetable mission and created a favorable environment for builders and private sectors not only from India, but also from abroad to invest and build.

When was the last time India experienced railways increased its capex three times in three years when it comes to railways? India was running on a signalling system that was 100 years old and no one cares. The route from Delhi to Kolkata was super jammed and urgently needed upgrades. But nobody cared about it. None of the northeastern capitals, except Guwahati, were linked to the rest of the country. Today, six out of seven are connected to Agartala and many others shaving direct trains to Delhi and other major cities such as Bengaluru and Mumbai.

A lot of projects were awarded under the previous establishment, money was disbursed and a big hoopla was orchestrated, while for years and years nothing significant happened on the ground. But Indians see that order completely revised in the current administration, for which it should be very happy, satisfied and excited. People often say that during the tenure of UPA-2, all these projects were launched by PM Modi. What they do not realize is that when UPA-2 left, most of these projects either turned npas or were on the brink. These projects were sabotaged and the current government had to bring them back to rolling roads with Nitin Gadkari.

Foreign Policy

Now, when we talk about foreign policy, it can be said that it is no longer so polite in judgment. And the dampener is the growing hostility between neighboring countries towards India. In particular, Nepal and Bhutan. Yes, many may not know that a large Bhutanese population is irritated by Indian intervention and dominance over them. So much so that many political analysts have announced that two factions-those who are pro-India and those who are not-will fight for the next elections in Bhutan.

Defence and Security

India has internal security and overall strength and the well-being of the armed forces to discuss when discussing defence. As far as internal security is concerned, India is believed to have seen tremendous success in containing Naxalism, stopping its spread and also bringing down separatist and insurgency movements in northeastern countries. This is why AFSPA has been revoked or reduced in some North East India states and territories. Yes, J&K was undoubtedly a boiler. However, if the Indian Constitution does not repeal Sections 370 and 35A, no significant and lasting good can be achieved. The hardline approach therefore appears to be only a viable option for dealing with extremists and terrorists.

As far as the well-being of the armed forces is concerned, an army major states that, "Whatever government is in the centre, there has never been a good relationship with the armed forces. That's because no government can ever do everything the armed forces expect it to do. "Therefore, the assessment of armed forces support is relative. Did the present government do better for Indian Jawaans and Rakshaks than the previous government of UPA-2? Many think the answer is a big yes. With amazing support from the armed forces for their actions on the ground against the militants and repeated cross-fire and shelling at the border, the way in which the actions of the present government are really unprecedented.

Women In India

Now let's talk about women's improvement. Under the Ujjwala Yojana, the government has already distributed 4.65 crore-free LPG cylinders to poor families who used coal and wood choolahs, leaving them to breathe, eradicating many from possible lung infections, attenuating vision and even cancer. And who is this movement's biggest beneficiary? Females. The same applies to the movement of the toilet. The government claims that more than 7.7 million new household toilets have been built. And I don't think so. But if they claim that, at least half of that number should be true. That would not be a small or trivial achievement in any measure. Again, it's the women who will most benefit from the toilets.

Using this two-pronged strategy, PM Modi has tried beautifully to reach out to the pan India women by directly addressing the problems they face every day.

Employment

When naysayers say PM Modi hasn't given the jobs he promised, just ask those people a question that apparently nobody could ever answer. Under the current Mudra Yojana government, more than 12 crore individuals from SC / ST / OBC communities were granted loans of up to 10 lakhs to run their own business. Now that 12 crore business loans have been granted, can it be wrong to assume that at least one person has created a job for each of these companies? That's the minimum number. The actual number should be over. So, it's simple math. Those who don't think the number can go to Mudra Yojana's web portal and see the results for themselves.

If Not Modi For PM In 2019, Then Who?

India has a rich, inexperienced man who thinks he deserves to be a prime minister because he was born into a prime minister family. Also, because he wears a white Kurta almost every time he is in India, he thinks he looks like a mass commoner. So he thinks it's his privilege, his fate, his right to be Prime Minister. Even though he has been an elected Member of Parliament for Amethi since 2004, he has the audacity to promise that he would turn Amethi into Singapore if he were elected again. Do you think he's? You can choose. I know where I'm. Move on. We have an archaic, clever and self-centered politician named Didi, under whose rule we hear about a new riot in West Bengal. A woman under whom in all socio-economic metrics West Bengal, once one of India's most prosperous states, has begun to slip behind most major states. Do I want the same chaos in pan-India? You know my reply. And finally, we have a proven, learned and experienced Chief Minister of Telangana, who is a great choice. But it's a big one, but! He would have to go for a coalition with figures such as Didi and many others from BSP and SP to become PM. And that's just not in this country's best interest. Under UPA rule, we have seen what happens when such a coalition comes to power despite being led by a relatively honest and dedicated PM.

So, Who Am I Supposed To Vote For?

PM Modi, to be true, didn't do that bad either. In particular, when you juxtapose him against all his predecessors, I'd say he did a better job than most of them. PM Modi is therefore the man I want to see leading my country also after 2019. And, that's why I'll vote for him. First, because I think he did a fairly good job. Secondly, I don't see a better choice.

9 781798 913031